A Practical Guide
To
Obtaining Probate
Peter Wade

Emerald Guides

Straightforward Publishing

© Peter Wade 2018

ISBN: 978-1-84716-866-5

Printed by 4edge Ltd www.4edge.co.uk

Cover design by Bookworks Derby
Whilst every effort has been made to ensure that the information contained within this book is correct at the time of going to press, the author and publisher can take no responsibility for the errors or omissions contained within.

CONTENTS

INTRODUCTION

The saying goes that we can avoid everything except death and taxes. Maybe probate has the unique distinction of dealing with both these activities. We cannot avoid death but we can avoid taxes.

The proper regulation of one's estate can certainly minimise inheritance tax and maybe get rid of it entirely.

Life becomes more complicated by the day but it is possible without running up excessive legal fees to prepare a valid will and as an executor to undertake probate of someone's estate without legal help.

My definition of probate is very high-class administration. We are capable of doing it if we follow the checklists assiduously and keep a note of everything we do. If every piece of paper is accounted for and filed properly then probate should not be too difficult. With the advent of the Internet these things are more easily undertaken by the organised amateur.

The minimum you will need is
1. Telephone
2. Computer
3. Somewhere to file all the letters.

I have attempted to take you through a typical probate transaction and to supply you with checklists, addresses, telephone numbers, and website addresses and draft letters.

I have tried to keep the text uncluttered by keeping the non-essential items to the appendixes. There will be notes in the text where these things can be found.

I purchased my first house by using a book although I did have the advantage of working in the legal department of a local authority. I knew nothing about practical conveyancing. It was a famous consumer association guide and I still have that copy on my shelves even though it was about 33 years ago. I am a great believer in *'how to books'*. They can at the very least take out this mystique of what the professionals try to wrap up as being very complicated indeed.

Wills and probate is not brain surgery but you have to follow a procedure precisely to get it right. You can save thousands in legal fees,)which are due to jump quite dramatically in 2019 depending on the value of the estate)

WRITING YOUR OWN WILL

Everyone over the age of 18 should make a will. Although in the public's view making a will is a straightforward matter it can have devastating effect if not written and executed properly and also if there is no will.

The safest advice is to always get a competent person to draw up and have a will executed for you. You can then rest assured that your wishes will be carried out in the event of your death.

Also if you execute it whilst you are fit and well there is less likelihood of it being overturned by beneficiaries claiming that you were not competent to do it.

If you are in any doubt about your own ability to draw up and execute a will you should get a solicitor to do it for you. At the very least your beneficiaries will be able to sue the solicitor in the event of him or her being incompetent or your beneficiaries missing out because of negligence. If you draw up a poor will they will only be able to regret for the rest of their lives that you had not taken competent legal advice which comes relatively cheaply for a straightforward will.

I often claim that I would happily pay the solicitor's fee for a will to be drawn up were I to be the beneficiary. So far I have not been called upon to pay up on that promise as no one has indicated that they want to make me a beneficiary.

As a practising probate lawyer I see a lot of heartache amongst families when they think the will has not been drawn up properly or they think they can overturn the will because the testator was not mentally capable. Unfortunately the chance of inheriting does not bring out the best in people. Also families in those circumstances do not seem to enjoy themselves more than when they are falling out over money. We all believe that it would not happen in our family as we are not so petty and mercenary but in my experience no one is exempt.

We would much rather total strangers get part of the estate than let "undeserving" members of our own family.

Occasionally I get well meaning 'know alls' who say I am not paying your fees as everything will go to the wife when I die. That is partially true but intestacy trusts in favour of the children may arise which can tear apart a family. I suppose this boast is to prove how clever the speaker is.

I counter if I am in a difficult mood by saying: yes you deprive me of my fee but you are taking a risk that in the event of your joint death and intestacy your sister in law will inherit your estate. I have no idea whether the speaker has a sister in law but it usually encourages them to dip into their wallet to pay my fee for a properly drawn up Will.

We all have someone to whom we do not wish to leave our estate even if it's only the taxman. Or, on intestacy, ultimately the State. If you leave it to the cats' home provided it is a charity you save the tax and keep it out of the Chancellor's hands. A satisfying outcome

WHY MAKE A WILL?

If you do not have a will then your estate will be distributed in accordance with the rules of intestacy. Intestacy means when there is no will. A testator is the maker of a will.

Apart from limited circumstances you have freedom to leave your estate to whomever you like unlike some other legal systems such as in France.

You are entitled to go to the stationers and use a will form. The only problem with that is that it may work but any mistake in execution will invalidate your wishes.

Everyone should make a will and think about updating it regularly as your circumstances change.

Finally, this book deals with probate in England and Wales. For information concerning Scotland:

www.scotcourts.gov.uk/taking-action/dealing-with-a-deceased's-estate-in-scotland

For Northern Ireland:

www.nidirect.gov.uk/applying-probate

****

CHAPTER 1

PRACTICAL WILL DRAFTING

Revocation of Wills

There are two main ways that you can revoke your will: by writing a new one; a formal declaration of all previous wills, by deliberately destroying the will.

Also the Testator must intentionally destroy the will or order someone else to destroy it in his presence.

There are statutory rules as to revocation of wills, and the most important ones being marriage and divorce.

Inheritance tax

Inheritance Tax is a tax on the estate (the property, money and possessions) of someone who's died.

There's normally no Inheritance Tax to pay if either:

- the value of the estate is below the £325,000 threshold
- a person leaves everything to their spouse or civil partner, a charity or a community amateur sports club

If the estate's value is below the threshold a person will still need to report it to HMRC. If a person gives away their home to their children (including adopted, foster or stepchildren) or grandchildren the threshold can increase to £450,000.

If a person is married or in a civil partnership and their estate is worth less than the threshold, any unused threshold can be added to their partner's threshold when they die. This means their threshold can be as much as £900,000.

Inheritance Tax rates

The standard Inheritance Tax rate is 40%. It's only charged on the part of the estate that's above the threshold.

Example An estate is worth £500,000 and the tax-free threshold is £325,000. The Inheritance Tax charged will be 40% of £175,000 (£500,000 minus £325,000).

The estate can pay Inheritance Tax at a reduced rate of 36% on some assets if a person leaves 10% or more of the 'net value' to charity in their will.

Reliefs and exemptions

Some gifts given while alive may be taxed after death. Depending on when a person gave the gift, 'taper relief' might mean the Inheritance Tax charged is less than 40%.

Other reliefs, such as Business Relief, allow some assets to be passed on free of Inheritance Tax or with a reduced bill.

A person should contact the Contact the Inheritance Tax and probate helpline on 0300 123 1072 about Agricultural Relief if their estate includes a farm or woodland.

Passing on a home

A person can pass a home to their husband, wife or civil partner when they die. There's no Inheritance Tax to pay if they do this.

If a person leaves the home to another person in their will, it counts towards the value of the estate.

If a person owns their home (or a share in it) their tax-free threshold can increase to £450,000 if:

- they leave it to their children (including adopted, foster or stepchildren) or grandchildren
- the estate is worth less than £2 million

Giving away a home before a person dies

There's normally no Inheritance Tax to pay if a person moves out and lives for another 7 years.

If a person wants to continue living in their property after giving it away, they will need to:

- pay rent to the new owner at the going rate (for similar local rental properties)
- pay their share of the bills
- live there for at least 7 years

they do not have to pay rent to the new owners if both the following apply:

- they only give away part of your property
- the new owners also live at the property

If a person dies within 7 years

If a person dies within 7 years of giving away all or part of their property, their home will be treated as a gift and the 7 year rule applies.

Gifts

There's usually no Inheritance Tax to pay on small gifts a person makes out of their normal income, such as Christmas or birthday presents. These are known as 'exempted gifts'.

There's also no Inheritance Tax to pay on gifts between spouses or civil partners. A person can give them as much as they like during their lifetime, as long as they live in the UK permanently.

Other gifts count towards the value of the estate.

People a person gives gifts to will be charged Inheritance Tax if they give away more than £325,000 in the 7 years before their death.

What counts as a gift

A gift can be:

- anything that has a value, such as money, property, possessions
- a loss in value when something's transferred, for example if a person sells their house to their child for less than it's worth, the difference in value counts as a gift

Exempted gifts

A person can give away £3,000 worth of gifts each tax year (6 April to 5 April) without them being added to the value of the estate. This is known as the 'annual exemption'.

A person can carry any unused annual exemption forward to the next year - but only for one year.

Each tax year, they can also give away:

- wedding or civil ceremony gifts of up to £1,000 per person (£2,500 for a grandchild or great-grandchild, £5,000 for a child)

- normal gifts out of income, for example Christmas or birthday presents - they must be able to maintain your standard of living after making the gift
- payments to help with another person's living costs, such as an elderly relative or a child under 18
- gifts to charities and political parties

A person can use more than one of these exemptions on the same person - for example, they could give your grandchild gifts for her birthday and wedding in the same tax year.

Small gifts up to £250

A person can give as many gifts of up to £250 per person as they want during the tax year as long as they have not used another exemption on the same person.

The 7 year rule

If there's Inheritance Tax to pay, it's charged at 40% on gifts given in the 3 years before a person dies. Gifts made 3 to 7 years before death are taxed on a sliding scale known as 'taper relief'.

Years between gift and death	Tax paid
less than 3	40%
3-4	32%
4-5	24%
5-6	16%
6-7	8%
7 or more	0%

Gifts are not counted towards the value of the estate after 7 years.

When someone living outside the UK dies

If their permanent home ('domicile') is abroad, Inheritance Tax is only paid on their UK assets, for example property or bank accounts they have in the UK. It's not paid on 'excluded assets' like:

- foreign currency accounts with a bank or the Post Office
- overseas pensions
- holdings in authorised unit trusts and open-ended investment companies

There are different rules if a person has assets in a trust or government gilts, or they are a member of visiting armed forces.

When you will not count as living abroad

HMRC will treat a person as being domiciled in the UK if they either:

- lived in the UK for 15 of the last 20 years
- had their permanent home in the UK at any time in the last 3 years of their life

Double-taxation treaties

An executor might be able to reclaim tax through a double-taxation treaty if Inheritance Tax is charged on the same assets by the UK and the country where a person lived.

Post Death Planning

DEED OF VARIATION

Within the two-year period after the death the will can effectively be rewritten to take advantage of the nil-rate Inheritance Tax band. This is made by Deed of Family arrangement. All the beneficiaries must agree to this.

SUGGESTED PRECEDENT WILL CLAUSES

COMMENCEMENT: Name and address of Testator

This is the last will and testament of me ^^^^^^^ of ^^^^^^^ in the County of ^^^^^-

Formal revocation of all previous wills

I REVOKE all former Wills and Testamentary dispositions made by me-Funeral arrangements

I WISH that my body be buried/cremated-

Appointment of sole executor who is usually wife/ husband who is also sole beneficiary

I APPOINT my ^^^^ to be my sole Executor/Executrix and I GIVE AND BEQUEATH to ^^^^^ all my property both real and personal whatsoever and wheresoever absolutely PROVIDED that ^^^^^^ survives me by at least thirty days but if my said ^^^^ shall not so survive me I DIRECT that the remaining clauses hereof shall take effect-

Appointment of executor and alternative executor if first one predeceases

(1) I APPOINT my ^^^^ ("my ^^^^") to be the sole executor ^^^ of this Will but if that appointment fails (because ^^^^ dies before me or before proving the Will or is unable or unwilling to act or for any other reason) I APPOINT ^^^^^ of ^^^^^^ and ^^^^^^ of ^^^^^ to be the executors and trustees of the Will-

IN THIS WILL and any Codicil to it the expression "my Trustees" means its trustees for the time being or (where the context requires) my personal representatives for the time being-

ANY POWERS given to the trustees of this Will (by the Will or any Codicil to it or by the general law) may be exercised by my Trustees before the administration of my estate is complete and even before a grant or representation has been obtained-

Appointment of professional firm to be executors
NB charging clause

(1) I APPOINT the partners at the date of my death in the firm of ^^^^^^^^^^^ of ^^^^^^^^^^^^^ or the firm which at that date has succeeded to and carries on its practice and I EXPRESS the wish that one and only one of those partners (or

if the appointment of ^^^^ fails for any reason to take effect then two and only two of them) shall prove the Will and act initially it its trusts-

(2) IN THIS WILL the expression "my Trustees" means my Executors and Trustees of this Will and of any trust arising under it-

(3) ANY POWERS given to the trustees of this Will (by the Will or any Codicil to it or by the general law) my be exercised by my Trustees before the administration of my estate is complete and even before a grant or representation has been obtained-

Appointment of solicitors

(1) I APPOINT as my Executors and Trustees ^^ and the partners at the date of my death in the firm of ^^^^^^^^^ of ^^^^^^^^^ or the firm which at that date has succeeded to and carries on its practice and I EXPRESS the wish that one and only one of those partners (or if the appointment of ^^^^ fails for any reason to take effect then two and only two of them) shall prove the Will and act initially in its trusts-

(2) IN THIS WILL the expression "my Trustees" means my Executors and Trustees of this Will and of any trust arising under it-

(3) ANY POWERS given to the trustees of this Will by the Will or any Codicil to it or by the general law) may be exercised by my Trustees before the administration of my estate is

complete and even before a grant or representation has been obtained-

NORMAL APPOINTMENT OF EXECUTORS

(1) I APPOINT ^^^^^^ and ^^^^^ to be the Executors and Trustees of this my Will (hereinafter called "my Trustees)-

(2) IN THIS WILL the expression "my Trustees" means my Executors and Trustees of this Will and of any trust arising under it-

(3) ANY POWERS given to the Trustees of this Will (by the Will or any Codicil to it or by the general law) may be exercised by my Trustees before the administration of my estate is complete and even before a grant has been obtained-

I APPOINT ^^^^^ and his wife ^^^^^ and the survivor of them of ^^^^^^ and any person or persons appointed by him/her/them to act after his/her/their death or incapacity to be the guardians during minority of any children of mine who are the minors at the date of death of the survivor of me and my ^^^^^^-

Specific Legacies including personal chattels I GIVE AND BEQUEATH all my personal chattels as defined by Section 55(1) (x) of the Administration of Estates Act 1925 unto ^^^^^ absolutely-

I GIVE AND BEQUEATH all my personal chattels as defined by Section 55(1)(x) of the Administration of Estates Act 1925 unto my Trustees Upon Trust to dispose of the same as they in their absolute discretion shall think fit or in accordance with any note or memorandum which may be found amongst my papers at my death-

I GIVE AND BEQUEATH to ^^^^^ such of my personal chattels (as the same are defined by Section 55(1) (x) of the Administration of Estates Act 1925) as ^^^^^ may within two months of the date of my death select and I GIVE AND BEQUEATH all personal chattels remaining after ^^^^ has made ^^^^^ selection or the period for making such selection has expired to ^^^^-

Pecuniary legacies

I GIVE AND BEQUEATH the following specific legacies free of Inheritance Tax other fiscal impositions and of costs of transfer-

(1) ^^^^^^

(2) ^^^^^^

I GIVE AND BEQUEATH the following pecuniary legacies free of Inheritance Tax and other fiscal impositions:-

(1) To ^^^^^^^^ the sum of ^^^^^

(2) To ^^^^^^^^ the sum of ^^^^^

Pecuniary legacies to charities etc

I DECLARE that the receipt of the treasurer or other proper officer for the time being of ^^^^^ shall be a sufficient discharge to my Trustees for any legacy hereby given- *(Not necessary if using STEP provisions)*

(1) WITH REFERENCE to Section 31 of the trustee Act 1925 the words "may in all circumstances be reasonable" shall be omitted from paragraph 1 of subsection 1 and in substitution therefore the words "the Trustees may think fit" shall be inserted and the proviso at the end of subsection 1 shall be omitted-

(2) With reference to Section 32 of the Trustee Act 1925 provision A of subsection 1 shall be deemed to be omitted-

RECEIPT FROM CHARITY

THE RECEIPT of anyone purporting to be the treasurer or other proper officer of any charitable or other body to which any gift is made by (or under any provision of) this Will or any Codicil to it shall be a good discharge to my Trustees for the gift- *(Not necessary if STEP provisions being used)*

UNDERAGE BENEFICIARY

IF any legatee hereunder (whether specific or pecuniary) shall be a minor at my death my Trustees may if they think fit pay transfer or deliver the legacy to such legatee personally or to his parent or guardian and the receipt of such legatee notwithstanding his minority or of such parent or guardian shall be a sufficient discharge to my Trustees for such legacy who shall not be further concerned as to the application thereof-

Residuary estate

I GIVE DEVISE AND BEQUEATH all my real and the residue of my personal property whatsoever and wheresoever not hereinbefore specifically disposed of unto my Trustees upon trust to sell call in and convert the same into money with power to postpone the sale calling in and conversion thereof for so long as they in their absolute discretion shall think fit without being liable for loss-

I GIVE DEVISE AND BEQUEATH all my property both real and personal whatsoever and wheresoever unto my Trustees upon trust to sell call in and convert the same into money with power to postpone the sale calling in and conversion thereof for so long as they in their absolute discretion shall think fit without being liable for loss-

Duties of executors

MY TRUSTEES shall stand possessed of the net proceeds of such sale calling in and conversion as aforesaid and my ready money upon trust to pay thereout my debts funeral and testamentary expenses and all duty and taxes payable by reason of my death and after such payment in trust for my said ^^^^^^ absolutely and if ^^^^^^ shall predecease me then in trust for such of my children as shall survive me and attain the age of ^^^^ years and if more than one in equal shares absolutely-

PER STIRPES - Grandchildren taking the share their parent would have received if they had lived.

PROVIDED always that if any of my said children shall predecease me leaving issue living at my death who shall attain the age of ^^^ years such issue shall take by substitution per stirpes and if more then one in equal shares the share of my estate which his hers or their parent would have taken had he or she survived me-

RESIDUARY ESTATE

I GIVE all my property not otherwise disposed of by this my Will unto my Trustees upon trust to sell the same (with power to postpone sale) and out of the moneys to arise from such sale to pay my debts legacies my funeral and testamentary expenses and all duty and taxes payable by reason of my death and TO HOLD the residue of the said proceeds of sale in trust for ^^^^^ for ^^^^^ own use and benefit absolutely-

I GIVE all the residue of my estate (out of which shall be paid my funeral and testamentary expenses and my debts) and any property over which I have at my death any general power of appointment to my Trustees ON TRUST to sell call in and convert into money but with full power to postpone doing so for as long as they see fit without being liable for loss (and such estate and property and the property which currently represents it is referred to in this Will as "the Trust Fund")-

MY TRUSTEES shall hold the Trust Fund ON TRUST:-

> (1)　To pay its income to my said wife/husband for his/her life (but contingently on surviving me for twenty eight days and

(2) without becoming entitled to the income during that period except in that event) and subject to that :-

(3) Absolutely for such of my children as are alive at the death of the survivor of my said wife/husband and me and reach the age of ^^^ years and if more than one in equal shares PROVIDED that if any child of mine dies (in my lifetime or after my death) before attaining a vested interest but leaves a child or children alive at the death of the survivor of my said wife/husband my child and me who reach the age of ^^^^ years then such child or children shall take absolutely and if more than one in equal shares so much of the Trust Fund as that child of mine would have taken on attaining a vested interest-

I GIVE DEVISE AND BEQUEATH all the residue of my property both real and personal whatsoever and wheresoever not otherwise disposed of by this my Will and any Codicil hereto unto my Trustees upon trust for sale (with power to postpone such sale) to pay my debts funeral and testamentary expenses pecuniary legacies and all duties and other taxes payable by reason my death and to hold the net proceeds of sale upon trust for such of my children who survive me and attain the age of ^^^^ years and if more than one in equal shares absolutely PROVIDED ALWAYS that if any such child of mine shall die in my lifetime leaving issue who survive me and attain the age of ^^^ years then such issue shall take by substitution and more than one in equal shares per stirpes the share of my residuary estate which such deceased child of mine would have taken had he or she survived me and attained a vested interest under this my Will-

IF the foregoing provisions shall fail then my Trustees shall hold my residuary estate for ^^^^ and ^^^^ or the survivor or survivors of them in equal shares absolutely-

FAILURE OF GIFT / SHARE AND THE BALANCE TO GO TO RESIDUARY ESTATE

IF the trusts hereinbefore declared of and concerning any share of my residuary estate shall fail or determine then from the date of such failure or determination such shares shall accrue and be added to the other shares of my residuary estate in equal proportions and be held upon the like trusts and subject to the like powers and provisions as those affecting such other shares-

SURVIVORSHIP CLAUSE

EVERY person who would otherwise benefit under this Will but who fails to survive me for thirty days shall be deemed to have predeceased me for the purpose of ascertaining the devolution of my estate and the income from my estate during the period of thirty days from my death shall be accumulated and added to capital accordingly-

IN this Will or any Codicil to it the Standard provisions of the Society of Trust and Estate Practitioners (First Edition) shall apply-

Extension of executor's powers

MY TRUSTEES may in extension of the power of appropriation conferred on personal representatives by Section 41 of the Administration of Estates Act 1925 at any time at their discretion appropriate any part of my estate in its then actual condition or state of investments in or towards satisfaction of any legacy or any share in my estate without the necessity of obtain the consent of any person- *(Not necessary if STEP provisions are used)*

IN ADDITION to all other powers conferred by law my Trustees may at any time and from time to time raise the whole or any part of the vested contingent expectant or presumptive share or shares of any beneficiary hereunder and pay the same to or apply the same for the advancement maintenance education or otherwise howsoever for the benefit of such beneficiary-

ANY MONEYS requiring investment hereunder may be laid out in or upon the acquisition or security of any property of whatsoever nature and wheresoever situate to the intent that my Trustees shall have the same full and unrestricted power of investing in all respects as if they were absolutely entitled thereto beneficially- *(Not necessary if STEP provisions are used)*

POWER TO INSURE

MY TRUSTEES may insure any trust property (including property to which someone is absolutely entitled) for any amount (including an amount which allows for increases in costs and expenses through inflation or otherwise) against any risks (including the risk of any kind of consequential loss and the risk of public or third part liability) and may pay the premiums out of the income or the capital of the property insured or any other property held on the same trust-*(Not necessary if STEP provisions are used)*

I DECLARE that all income received after my death shall be treated and applied as income from whatever source or class of investment or property the same shall arise and even if the property in respect of which the income arises is sold for the payment of my debts or for other purposes and whatever the period may be in respect of which the income shall have accrued and that no property not actually producing income shall be treated as producing income-

CHARGING CLAUSE FOR PROFESSIONAL EXECUTORS

ANY TRUSTEE being a person engaged in a profession or business may act and be paid for all work done and time expended by himself or his firm in like manner as if he not having been appointed a Trustee hereof had been employed by the Trustees to do such work including acts of business which a Trustee not being engaged in such profession or business could have done personally-*(Not necessary if STEP provisions are used)*

Attestation clause

IN WITNESS whereof I have hereunto set my hand this   day of   Two Thousand ^^^^

SIGNED by the said ^^^^^^ the Testator/Testatrix as and for his/her last Will and testament in the presence of us both being present at the same time who at his/her request in his/her presence and in the presence of each other have hereunto subscribed our name as witnesses-

SIGNED by the above named ^^^^^^ in our joint presence and then by us in his-

SIGNED by the above named ^^^^ in our joint presence and then by us in hers-

SIGNED by the said ^^^^^ the Testatrix and as for her last Will and testament in the presence of us both present at the same time who at her request in her presence and in the presence of each other have hereunto subscribed our names as witnesses-

CODICILS

For Codicils........

IN all other respects I confirm my said Will

IN WITNESS whereof I have hereunto set my hand this   day of   Two Thousand and ^^^^^^
SIGNED by the said   ^^^^^^^^^^^^^^^^^^^^^^^^^^^^^^^^^^
)
As a Codicil to her Will in the joint presence of us both   )
Present at the same time who at her request in her
)
presence and in the presence of each other have   )
hereunto subscribed our names as witnesses-   )

TRUSTS

This is an area of law which can confuse the person in the street as it is a term that is used but not fully understood. It is in effect a legal device by which assets may be held on behalf of another.

The most basic trust is when a person under 18 who cannot give a valid receipt has assets held on his or her behalf until they reach the age of majority. Before the age of 18 the assets will be held by trustees and during that time the assets will be held on trust.

TRUSTEES

These are the people who have control of the property and take responsibility for the running of the trust.

BENEFICIARIES

These are the people who have the benefit of the trusts

WHY A TRUST SHOULD BE CREATED

➢ They are used for a variety of purposes

➢ To preserve assets which people retain in the family from being dissipated.

➢ As previously mentioned for land and other property to be held on behalf of a child who is incapable of holding such property in their own right. This arises because a minor cannot give a valid receipt for property.

➢ To create a pension fund

➢ To operate investments on behalf of others such as unit trusts

➢ As a tax saving device.

The situations where a trust might arise are as follows

Children

If you wish to make a gift to a child then a trust is necessary for legal reasons.

LIFE INTERESTS

If the testator wishes to leave property to another to be held by them during their lifetime and thereafter to another.

This would arise if say on a second marriage the testator wanted to allow his wife to reside in the matrimonial home and once she died the property to go to his children. The wife would be what is known as the life tenant and has the right to occupy the property during her life time. The wife therefore merely has the life interest and the property is held on trust for both her and the children

CONTINGENT INTERESTS

This is when a gift is given on a condition or contingent basis. The most common example is when a gift is made to someone until they achieve a certain age such as 21 or 25.

If a gift is given immediately is known as vested. When there is a condition it is contingent that is awaiting the passing of some event on this occasion the age of 21 or 25.

DIFFERENT TYPES OF TRUSTS

THE DISCRETIONARY TRUST

This can be used for tax planning purposes. It gives the trustees the right that is the discretion to deal with the property in the trust as they see fit.

THE ACCUMULATION AND MAINTENANCE TRUST

These are used for the benefit of children and grandchildren

THE INTEREST IN POSSESSION TRUST

This is where the beneficiaries have the right to use the property.

WHAT CAN THE TRUSTEES DO?

The trustees' powers come from a variety of sources being from the trust deed itself, Statutory authority and common law authority.

*

Appropriation

➢ Apportionment

➢ Investment

➢ Maintenance of a child

➢ Advancement of capital

➢ The relationship between trustees and beneficiaries

➢ Trusts and saving inheritance tax

****

CHAPTER 2

LASTING POWERS OF ATTORNEY AND ENDURING POWERS OF ATTORNEY

Lasting Powers of Attorney

Lasting Power of Attorney is a legal document which gives authority to another person to make decisions on your behalf. This is obviously someone you can trust to make decisions on your behalf. The Attorney you choose will be able to make decisions for you when you become lacking in mental capacity or simply no longer wish to do so

There are two types of Lasting Power of Attorney. There is:

- Property and Financial Lasting Power of Attorney, which allows your attorney to deal with your property and finances.
- Health and Welfare which allows your attorney to make care decisions on your behalf when you lack mental capacity to do so.

A Lasting Power of Attorney cannot be used until it is registered with the Office of the Public Guardian.

By having a Lasting Power of Attorney you are ensuring a safe way of having decisions made for you. The following reasons for this are:

- It has to be registered with the Office of the Public Guardian before it can be used
- You can choose someone to provide a 'certificate', which means they confirm that you understand the significance and purpose of what you're agreeing to. This is normally a solicitor or legal expert
- You can choose who gets told about your Lasting Power of Attorney when it is registered (so they have an opportunity to raise concerns). This may be a relative or someone close to you
- Your signature and the signatures of your chosen attorneys must be witnessed
- Your attorney(s) must follow the Code of Practice of the Mental Capacity Act 2005 and act in your best interests
- The Office of the Public Guardian provides helpful support and advice

The Mental Capacity Act 2005

The Attorney's must follow the code of the Mental Capacity Act 2005. Copies of this can be obtained from direct.gov.uk/mental capacity.

The main principles of the Act are:

- They must assume that you can make your own decisions
- They must help you to make as many decisions as you can

Your Attorney's must make decisions and act in your best interests when you are unable to make the decisions yourself.

What is Mental Capacity?

In everyday life we make decisions about various matters in our lives. We call this ability to make these decision 'Mental Capacity'

Some people may experience some difficulty in making decisions and this may be due to various reasons such as, a mental health problem, a learning disability or have had a stroke or brain injury.

The Mental Capacity Act of 2005 has more guidance on how to assess someone's ability to make decisions

This act covers decisions in areas such as property and financial affairs and health and welfare etc. It also covers everyday decisions such as personal care. The Act also sets out five principles that are the basis of the legal requirement of the Act.

Unless it can be proved otherwise, every adult has the right to make their own decisions. All available help must be given before they are deemed not to be able to make their own decisions.

Any decision made for a person who is unable to so for themselves must be done in their best interests. Any decisions made for someone else should not restrict their basic rights and freedoms.

The Court of Protection has the power to make decisions about whether someone lacks mental capacity. It can also appoint deputies to act and make decisions on behalf of someone who is unable to do so on their own.

Enduring Powers of Attorney (EPA's)

No more Enduring Powers of Attorney may be created after the 1st October 2008, but there are Enduring Powers of Attorney which are in existence and they are perfectly legally valid.

It is a legal document by which the Donor give the legal right to one or more Attorney's to manage the Donor's property and financial affairs.

The document allows the Attorney's to do anything that the Donor would have been able to do for themselves.

*

General Powers of Attorney

A General Power of Attorney can still be created but this ends when the Donor lacks mental capacity, but an Enduring Power of Attorney continues even once this capacity no longer exists.

Under an enduring Power of Attorney, once the Donor becomes mentally incapable the Attorney will need to apply to Register the Enduring Power of Attorney with the OPG.

Enduring Powers of Attorney were created under the Enduring Powers of Attorney Act 1985 which has been repealed by the Mental Capacity Act of 2005. The capacity to create an EPA was assumed to exist unless it was proven to the contrary.

If a person has mental capacity then Enduring Power of Attorney can be used like an Ordinary Power of Attorney. Once the mental capacity has lost this has to be registered.

Under an Enduring Power of Attorney, Attorney's may be appointed jointly or jointly and severally. Whereas with a single Attorney, that Attorney should sign on each occasion where two or more Attorneys are appointed they can be joint or joint and several. Jointly means both Attorney's need to sign on every occasion. Joint and Several means that either of the Attorneys could both sign but are not required to sign on each occasion. Both are not required to sign on each occasion.

Registration of an EPA

When an Attorney has reason to believe that the Donor has become mentally incapable he must apply to register the EPA.

Registration is made by completing the prescribed forms and giving notice to certain individuals who are entitled to receive notice of the intended registration.

Various parties are entitled to receive notice of intention to register and notice should be sent to:

- The Donor
- The Attorney's
- Close relatives of the Donor

There is a list of relatives to whom the notice should be given. Once up to three close relatives have been notified the provisions have been complied with.

The Difference Between Enduring Powers Of Attorney and Lasting Powers of Attorney

As stated, there cannot now be created an Enduring Power of Attorney, since the 30th September 2007.

With a Lasting Power of Attorney, it must contain names or persons who the donor wishes to be notified of any application and also must contain the Certificate that the donor understands the purpose of the instrument.

Decisions made under an LPA/EPA

Under an EPA the attorneys can do anything with the Donor's property and financial affairs, but cannot make decisions about the Donor's personal welfare.

Under an LPA the Attorney's can make decisions about property and financial affairs and personal welfare, including refusing consent to treatment.

The latter applies only if the Donor lacks, or that the Attorney reasonably believes that the Donor lacks mental capacity.

Who Can Create a Lasting Power of Attorney?

Anyone can create a Lasting Power of Attorney and it can also be described as the Capacity, that is those who are able make a Lasting Power of Attorney. The Donor (the person making the LPA) has to be at least 18 years of age and has to have the mental capacity to execute under the Mental Health Act 2005.

The definition of lack of capacity is if a person lacks capacity in relation to a matter if at the material time he is unable to make a decision for himself in relation to the matter because of an impairment or of a disturbance in the functioning of the mind or brain. This may be either a temporary or permanent disturbance. There is a presumption that a person can be assumed to have mental capacity unless it is established that he lacks capacity.

All persons over the age of 18 years of age are presumed to be capable of making their own decisions. The standard of proof is on a balance of probabilities. The Lasting Power of Attorney includes a certificate by a person of a prescribed description that at the time the Donor executes the instrument that;

- The Donor understood the purpose of the instrument and the scope of the authority conferred under it.

- No fraud or undue pressure is used to induce the Donor to create an LPA

- There is nothing else which would prevent an LPA from being created from the instrument.

The current Fees for Registering a Power of Attorney can be found on the Office of Public Guardian website.

The Lasting Power of Attorney can be cancelled at any time as long as the person giving it has mental capacity to cancel

What happens if there is no LPA?

If there is no LPA then an application will need to be made to the Court of Protection at considerably more cost and with no guarantee that the right person will be appointed as the Deputy as it is named.

Creating a Lasting Power of Attorney

The forms can be found on the Ministry of Justice website. The Registration must be done correctly and if there is a defect in the form may result in the refusal of the registration. Once the LPA has been signed errors cannot be simply corrected although the OPG may allow certain amendments.

Executing the LPA – it must be signed by the Donor, the Certificate provider and the Attorneys in the correct order.

Execution by the Donor or the Attorneys must take place in the presence of a witness.

Restrictions on who can act as a witness are:

• The Donor and the Attorney must not witness each other's signature.

It is also suggested that neither the Donor's spouse or civil partner witness the LPA.

CHAPTER 3

BEFORE THE GRANT OF PROBATE

Administration of the estate

This is a general term relating to the winding up of the estate. It has to be done whether there is a will and executors are appointed or if there is no will and an administrator takes over the duties of the winding up the estate. The estate is of course all the assets and liabilities of the deceased. The public tends to think of an estate as meaning only freehold land as in a landed estate. Lawyers of course mean all the deceased's worldly goods. Whether freehold leasehold or personal

Immediate steps

Registration of the death

Normally the lawyers will not be involved in the registration of the death but if you do any amount of probate you will be called upon to do it because there are no close relatives or the firm are the executors.

The responsibility of registering the death is usually upon a relative but any person present may undertake it. When the solicitor is the executor then he/ she can discharge the duty.

It must be registered in the district where the death took place or the body was found.

The death should be registered within five days but an extension can be granted.

The procedure is that the registrar will require a medical certificate of the cause of death on occasions this is sent directly to the registrar and all you need do is make an appointment.

The registrar will require details of the date and place of birth and whether or not the deceased was or had been married...

As a precaution if you hold the will make sure the names that you register are the same as the names on the will as you may have problems later on when making an application for probate.

You will have to personally check the details and sign together with paying the fee. Obtain further copies of the death certificate as necessary.

The death certificate is a certified copy of the entry of death on the register. Each copy will be £7.00 (can change between local authority areas).

Disposal of the body

It cannot be disposed off until the death has been registered and a green disposal certificate authorising whether it is a burial or cremation.

If the coroner is involved there may be delay in the registration of the death.

Any wishes by the deceased as to the disposal of the body is merely a wish and is not legally binding but most executors will respect the deceased's wishes

Funeral

It is not technically part of the executor's duties to arrange a funeral but the executor has the duty to dispose of the body. As he will be responsible for the costs out of the estate it is usual for the executor to at least be consulted.

The direct costs of the funeral such as church, cemetery and cremation fees will be testamentary and administration expenses but not refreshments for mourners. Any payment for those out of the estate will need the permission of the residuary beneficiaries.

Burial

The funeral director makes arrangement for the burial of the body. Bodies may be buried elsewhere with permission of the local authority.

Headstones may only be erected with the permission of the priest in charge there is no automatic right to a headstone. Again the cost of the headstone will not normally be regarded as a testamentary expense. Care should be taken before disposing of all the assets of the estate that sufficient money has been held back to pay for this at a later date. An estimate will be given but a margin should be retained as it is very embarrassing at a later date to have to ask the beneficiaries to pay when they think the estate has been wound up.

Dealing with assets where no grant is required

These include

1.   Nominated property

2.   Property held on a joint tenancy: this would include land, bank accounts and building society accounts. Joint shareholdings.

3.   Life policies written in trust. Although it can be transferred immediately it does not mean that it will not be subject to Inheritance tax if it comes within the tax limit.

Obtaining the will

Solicitors and banks will only normally produce the Will on production of the death certificate and authority from the executors.

Care should be taken that it is the last Will.

With the executors instructions you should send copies of the Will to the residuary beneficiaries.

Taking possession of the deceased persons estate

You should take possession of anything of a financial nature relating the deceased's estate which ranges from actual cash to title deeds.

It is good practice when receiving items from the relatives to produce a comprehensive checklist. Send a copy of the schedule to the relatives as soon as possible. This will form the basis of the estate account. Also it will resolve any future problems as you can quite rightly claim that you only have possession of the items that are on the checklist. Try not to take possession of items that will give you problems in storing as the beneficiaries will look to you to keep them safe. Give back all bags, cases etc as otherwise your office/home will end up looking like a left luggage office and you will never know if ever when or how to dispose of these items. They may turn out to be family heirlooms. If any items are collected during the administration, be absolutely scrupulous about asking for receipts before they leave your possession. If in doubt about anyone's authority or identity make sure you check it before parting with the items.

These are all precautions to keep down any potential complaints.

There is circumstance when assets may turn up later and an amended account can be submitted to HMRC. You should impress on the executors / administrators their duty to give a full and frank disclosure of the estate to HM Revenue and Customs, similarly with their duty to the beneficiaries.

The more detailed and evidential your account the less likely you are to have an enquiry from the revenue if all values are backed up by professional and current valuations your clients will have discharged their duties to the best of their abilities.

Practical considerations

1.   secure any freehold or leasehold property. Obtain keys arrange for them to be locked etc.

2.   disconnection or inform utilities such as water gas electricity.

3.   all deliveries have been stopped or post-redirected.

Insurance

Check there is an insurance policy in existence and contact insurance company about the interim arrangements.

Powers of Personal representatives before the grant

Executors

An executor's powers come from the death and the Will. The grant of probate is merely a confirmation to those powers. In reality the power is restricted by the fact that any other parties holding the assets will not release the money until a grant of probate has been produced.

Administrators

Their powers derive from the grant of administration, therefore they do not have the powers of an executor.

It is important that the administrator does not intermeddle with the estate as otherwise he will not be able to renounce afterwards.

Certain basic activities such as insuring the property and feeding animals would be regarded as necessary and not intermeddling.

Vesting

Property vests in the executor immediately but not with the administrator.

Obviously on the sale of property such as land the purchaser will expect to see the grant of probate even though it automatically vests in the executor.

Ascertaining the assets and liabilities.

Good practice is to use a checklist and examples as follows:

1.   Will

Where kept

Letter of Authority to release

Name & Address of Executors

1)   ....   2).........................

....

....

3)   ....   4).........................

....

1.   No Will

Entitlement to estate...

Name & Address of Administrators

1)...

....

....

2.   Particulars of Deceased

Full Name...

Alias..

Date of Death   ....   Date of Birth..............

Last Usual Address...

Married Status: Married / Single / Divorced / Widowed

Occupation...

Surviving Relatives:

Spouse [   ] Children [   ] Parents [   ]

Domicile:

England & Wales   [   ] Scotland [   ]

Wales   [   ]

National Insurance

Number...

Accountant:

Name...

Address...

Stockbroker / Financial Advisor

Name...

Address...

Bank Details

Name   ....   Account no.........

Address...

Joint Property Asset:

House] Bank a/c] Investments [

Description...

Joint Holder...

Joint Tenants   [   ]   Tenants in Common   [

Schedule of assets and debts

Asset	Probate Value £	Corrected Value £	Grant Registered	Proceeds £
Stocks Shares				
National Savings Certificates				
Building Society a/c				
Current a/c Bank				
Deposit a/c Bank				
Premium Bonds				
Life Policies Bonds				

Freehold Property				
Leasehold Property				

Debts

Creditor Name	Nature of Debt	Amount £	Corrected Amount £	Date Paid
Utilities				
Inland Revenue				
Funeral A/c				

This checklist can immediately form the basis of the estate account and can be split into assets and liabilities.

VALUING THE ESTATE

Letters should be sent to all holders of assets that need valuation

The letter should ask

1.   Details of the asset i.e. how much is in the account.

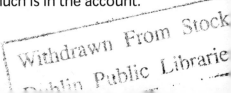

2.   Any income that has accrued since death such as interest.

3.   Send a copy of the death certificate as banks will normally expect to see this.

4.   Ask for any forms which may become necessary to sell or close the account for signature by the executors after the grant of probate.

Bank and building society accounts

You will need to ask the following

1.   Balance plus interest if any
2.   Details of any other accounts
3.   Any items held on safe deposit.
4.   Details of any standing orders or any money received after date of death which may need to be refunded such as pension payments.
5.   You may need to borrow the IHT liability so ask them for any details that they might want.

Banks and building societies are more liberal about this and it is better to ask for money in the existing account if this is possible. If not a loan will need to be set up.

Stocks and shares

A list of all the shares should be set up. You need to be meticulous with the actual share certificates that you take possession of. Make sure you create a schedule and get the executors or informants to sign the list by way of confirmation that is all they have given you.

People are exceedingly lax with certificates. And arguments can arise later as to what originals you possess

Obtain valuation from a stockbroker for which a fee is payable. Take instructions from the beneficiaries if at some date they wish them to be sold.

National Savings

Make application to the Director of Savings to obtain a valuation and forms to cash the holdings if necessary.

Building society accounts

Similar letter as to bank.

Social security /Pension

Letter to local office ask for balances or amounts owed.

Private Pension scheme

As above

Life Assurance

Obtain value of policy

Obtain Claim form

Land

An estate agent's valuation. Unless it is a farm then a full professional valuation as you may be claiming a relief.

It is possible for the executors to give a valuation but the district valuer will be keen to be involved. Also you need to be aware that for Capital Gains Tax purposes that the value at death will be the start value for the beneficiaries if the property is sold at a later date or transferred by way of assent. It is therefore important to get this right even if no IHT is payable. It will be much more difficult many years later to do a back calculation. Remind beneficiaries of this so that you are not involved in hours of abortive work at some future date.

Funeral expenses

It is good practice to ask the holders of any funds to pay the funeral account. This has a double effect. It removes any embarrassment by the beneficiaries as the funeral director may contact them. It helps the funeral directors cash flow and cuts down any further administration by you.

Council Tax

There will be an exemption so write to the council immediately if the property is empty.

All other debts

Write and ask for accounts and state you will pay them once probate has been granted and the funds are available.

HM Customs and Excise

If the deceased had an accountant supply him with a copy of death certificate and ask for his requirements.

Statutory advertisements

By advertising a personal representative will discharge his duty for payment of accounts not known by him.

Searches

Should you do a bankruptcy search against the deceased? Similarly you may wish to take a bankruptcy search against any large beneficiaries as if you pay them the money and not their trustee in bankruptcy you may not have discharged your duty.

The Executors may be liable if property / money is handed to someone who is bankrupt. They cannot give a valid receipt

Taxation of the Estate

There are three taxes that could affect the estate.
1. Income Tax
2. Capital Gains Tax
3. Inheritance Tax

The personal representatives are under a duty to deal with the deceased's tax affairs, and settle any outstanding liabilities and claim any rebates that may be necessary.

If the estate is large enough they will have to complete and submit the Inheritance Tax Account before probate or Letters of Administration will be granted.

In the event of inheritance tax having to be paid this will have to be paid before the grant is made.

Income tax

A return must be made to HMRC with the deceased's income up to the date of the death. The personal representative therefore should write to HMRC firstly to report the death and secondly to obtain a return to discover whether any tax may be due or owed to the estate.

The estate is entitled to the full personal reliefs for the tax year in question regarding the death.

Income received

Income received during the administration period.

There may be income that is being received during the administration period, such as salary, rent, dividends and interest on any investments.

Estate Income

This is income received during the administration period and finishes on the day when the value of the residuary estate is calculated for distribution purposes.

The personal representative must pay income tax received during the administration period although there are no personal reliefs.

The only advantage is that the estate in not liable for a higher rate tax which is currently 40%. There is relief for any interest paid, and may arise as a result of obtaining allowance for the inheritance tax.

Capital Gains Tax

The personal representatives must settle any Capital gains tax payable on any gains made during the deceased's lifetime. There is no Capital gains tax liability just as a result of the death and the personal representatives and beneficiaries ultimately are treated as acquiring the assets on the deceased's death, at their market value at the date of death.

It can therefore be very important to have a correct valuation of assets even though inheritance tax may not be payable, this will be the starting point for the beneficiaries in any future capital gains tax liability.

Inheritance Tax

As we have seen, Inheritance tax is payable on the value of all the property that the deceased owned, up to the date of death. This includes property passing under his will, or under the intestacy rules as well as property held under a joint tenancy and nominated property. There are important exemptions, depending on who is the beneficiary, and no inheritance tax will be payable in the following circumstances.

- Spouse of a deceased
- A Charity
- A Political party
- Some national bodies such as museums and art galleries

Inheritance tax may be avoided is there is business property or agricultural property relief and inheritance tax may be payable if the deceased has died within seven years of making a lifetime gift. There is however tapering relief over the seven year period.

Raising funds for paying the IHT on the personality

It is possible to pay instalments on land but not on the personal possessions. This has to be paid before the grant is made so you may have to borrow the tax before you have access to the funds.

Once borrowed or accessed the cheque will usually be in favour of HMRC.

Building Societies

This could be your best source of funds as they may allow you to have a cheque with only forms signed by the executors.

Direct Payment Scheme

Banks are now more susceptible to paying the money direct to HMRC which is only fair as it is the deceased's money and therefore the estates.

Beneficiary

Some beneficiaries may be able to pay IHT out of their own resources so as not to incur interest. Please ask.

****

CHAPTER 4

MAKING THE APPLICATION-AFTER THE GRANT

The grant of representation is the official document issued by the court and is conclusive proof that the administrators or executors legal authority to deal with the estate.

Registration

The form for application for probate is form PA1. (In Scotland it is form C1 applying for confirmation). When making an application for probate you need to state how many office copies you require. At £215 pounds (2018/19) for the Grant and 50pence each sealed office copy you should obtain enough for you to send copies to collect in the estate expeditiously. There is no fee if the estate is under £5,000. Note, as stated in the introduction, probate fees are under review and are set to change in April 2019.

If you need help with the process of applying for probate or advice on inheritance tax you should call the Probate and Inheritance Tax helpline on 0300 123 1072. Probate forms should be sent to your local Probate Registry. You can find out details by contacting:

https://courttribunalfinder.service.gov.uk

Swear an oath

The probate office will send you an oath and details of how to arrange an appointment. You'll need to swear the oath at either:

- the office of a commissioner for oaths (usually a solicitor)

- a local probate office

The oath is a promise that the information you've given is true to the best of your knowledge.

You should get the grant through the post within 10 working days of swearing the oath.

If it's not possible to issue a grant, the Probate Service will explain why in writing.

Once you have the grant of probate it is good practice to send a photocopy to the executors/ beneficiaries to prove you have probate. Make it clear it is not an office copy as otherwise they will start using it for their own purposes and will be very disappointed when they get turned down by banks etc.

Whilst registering the grant you should send any claim form along so as to transfer withdraw or sell the assets. These should have been signed in readiness by the executors.

Deposit

As money comes in over and above what you need to settle immediate debts you should be putting the funds on deposit. If in a separate interest bearing account this will assist as you will not have to calculate the interest payable if it has been on deposit throughout the administration.

Realising the Assets

The most urgent matter may be paying off the IHT loan

Clearing the tax liabilities

Complete the tax return form R27 or R40 You should complete the tax return form for the period from the previous 6 April to the date of death.

Clearing the IHT position

The personal representatives may have given their own estimate of the value. As previously mentioned this value could have an effect on future tax for the beneficiaries Capital gains tax purposes. If the property is well below the IHT limit then the value of the land should be put in at as high a valuation as possible.

If the property that is subject to IHT is sold later for a lower figure than the probate value agreed then, if within three years of the date of death, you will be able to claim IHT loss relief.

Payment on account

If you have elected to pay by instalments, the instalment within six months after the end of the month on which the death occurred any tax outstanding is subject to interest.

Corrective account

If there is any variation on the agreed figures after the estate has been settled then a corrective account can be submitted for an overpayment or underpayment. If only minor then it may be acceptable to do this by letter and an assessment will be issued.

Clearance certificate.

Once all IHT has been paid and before final distribution you should obtain a clearance certificate form the capital taxes Offices on an IHT30. This will give the personal perspectives protection against any further claims.

If further assets become available obviously they should be declared

Instalment Option - Property

The personal representatives may elect to pay tax by instalments of up to ten equal instalments per year over ten years on land, certain securities and businesses.

Capital Gains tax

No charge to capital Gains tax arises on death. The assets are deemed to have been acquired at their market value at that date. When the asset is transferred to the beneficiaries they are deemed to have acquired the assets at the value at death. If there is a chargeable gain during the administration after claiming their allowances it will be subject to 40 per cent tax.

HMRC Charge

Whilst there is tax outstanding HMRC have a charge against those assets.

Distribution of the estate

EXECUTOR'S YEAR-Personal representatives have a year from the date of death before the beneficiaries can call upon them to distribute any part of the estate this is called the executors' year.

Personal representatives should protect themselves before distributing the estate.

The problems that could arise are an Outstanding tax liabilities this could include IHT, CGT and Income Tax. Obtain clearance certificates for all those:

Outstanding Debts

Place statutory advert if in doubt. Ones to look out for are funeral expenses and the headstone which may be placed later.

Unknown beneficiaries

Such as all the grandchildren these include both legitimate and illegitimate relatives.

Rectification action

There is a possibility that the will might be rectified within the first six months. Any action after six months requires leave of the court and the personal representatives are protected.

Family provision claims

Again if within the six months there may be a family provision claim.

Variation or disclaimer

Any deed of family arrangement could mean that a beneficiary will not accept a gift and disclaimer cannot be made once a beneficiary has accepted the gift.

Specific Problems - Dead Beneficiaries

If a beneficiary has died before the testator prima facie the gift will lapse unless the gift was of the whole or part of the residue in which case it will pass on to the person's estate.

Bankrupt beneficiaries.

It might be good practice to search against the beneficiaries as if any gift should be paid to the trustee in bankruptcy, the personal representatives need a valid receipt.

Which property pays the tax?

The Will should provide this

Specific Gift

This will entitle the beneficiary to all income and interest on that item since death it still does not become the property of the beneficiary until it has been vested in them

Assents of land.

This transfers the land to the beneficiaries. Now an AS1

Although no stamp duty you still have to complete an SDLT form.

Memorandum of the assent should be endorsed on the probate. This is obviously not so important now that land is registered as it would be difficult to try and transfer the same piece of land twice without becoming immediately aware of it!

FORMALITIES TO TRANSFER VARIOUS ASSETS

Personal chattels etc

By delivery no set method may be by conduct writing or verbally.

Bank account

Written instructions to bank or by cheque to beneficiary

National savings certificate etc

Withdrawal forms

Stocks and shares

Share or stock transfer forms.

Registered/Unregistered land

AS1

****

Schedule of Standard Probate Letters

(See overleaf)

1.   Letter to Debtors

2.   Letter to Creditors

3.   Letter to Bank applying for payment of Funeral Account

4.   Letter to Bank applying for payment of Inheritance Tax

5.   Letter to Capital Taxes re Inheritance Tax

6.   Letter to Probate Registry for Grant of Probate

7.   Letter to Bank or Building Society collecting funds

8.   Authority for receiving money

9.   Letter to Registrar to transfer shares

10.   Letter paying bills from the Estate

11.   Letter to Beneficiaries with statement for approval

12.   Letter sending Pecuniary Legacy

13.   Receipt for Pecuniary Legacy *(on behalf of ....)*

14.   Receipt for Pecuniary Legacy

15.   Letter to Beneficiary

16.   Receipt for Beneficiary

17.   Instruction sheet for a Will

****

STANDARD LETTERS

Please note that these are for guidance only and may change depending on the circumstances.

1.   Letter to Debtors

Any date

Address

Dear Sirs

Re   *Name* – deceased
      Description
      Account No:

We enclose certified copy of the Death Certificate of the above and should be obliged if you would let us know the amount outstanding to the credit of this account including interest accrued but not credited at the date of death.

Probate will be registered with you in due course.

If you have any form or if you require authority for the Executors to sign to let us have any proceeds, repayments or monies due to the Estate could you please let us have such forms.

Alternatively please confirm at this stage exactly what authority you will require. This should save delays once Probate has been granted.

Yours faithfully

2.   Letter to Creditors

Any date

Customer Services
Address

Dear Sirs

Re   *Name*   –   deceased
Account Number:

We act on behalf of the Estate of the above unfortunately .... died on the .... we enclose a copy of the death certificate for your information and retention.

We would be obliged if you would kindly forward all future accounts to ourselves. We are currently making application for Probate, once this is available we will pay all outstanding accounts.

Yours faithfully

3.   Letter to Bank Applying for Payment of Funeral Account

Any date

Bank/Building Society
Address

Dear Sirs

Re   *Name*   –   deceased
**   Address:**
**   Account No:**

As you are aware we act on behalf of the Estate of the Late
....

We enclose a copy of the funeral account and we would be obliged if it is at all possible for you to draw a cheque in favour of .... to pay this account. If you require any forms to be signed by our client please do not hesitate to contact us.

Your assistance is appreciated

Yours faithfully

4.   Letter to Bank applying for payment of Inheritance Tax

Any date

Bank
Address

Dear Sirs

Re .... **–** **deceased**
Account No: ....

As you are aware we act for the Estate of the Late ....

There is a small amount of £........... due for Inheritance Tax and we would be obliged if it is at all possible for you to draw a cheque in favour of Her Majesty's Revenue and Customs to pay the amount due.

If you require any forms to be signed by the Executors please do not hesitate to contact us.

Your assistance is appreciated.

Yours faithfully

5.   Letter to Capital Taxes re Inheritance Tax

Any date

Capital Taxes Offices

Dear Sirs

Re   *Name* – deceased

We take this opportunity of enclosing the following:

1. A cheque in the sum of £??????? - the total amount of Inheritance Tax due

2. IHT200

3. D1

4. D7

5. D10

6. D13

7. D17

8. D18

We would be obliged if the D18 could be receipted and returned to us in due course.

Yours faithfully

6. Letter to Probate Registry for Grant of Probate

Any date

Ipswich District Probate Registry
8 Arcade Street
Ipswich
Suffolk IP1 1EJ

Dear Sirs

Re   Name – deceased

We enclose the following to lead to a Grant of Probate of the will of the above:

1. Oath for Executors

2. Will dated ?????

3. *Form IHT205 signed by the Executors*

    or

4. *D18*

5. Cheque in the sum of £????

We await hearing from you once Probate has been granted.

Yours faithfully

7. Letter to Bank or Building Society Collecting Funds

Any date
Bank/Building Society
Address

Dear Sirs

Re *Name* **deceased**

Account No: ....

We take this opportunity of enclosing the following:

1. Office Copy Probate – kindly return as soon as possible

2. Authority Letter/Withdrawal form

We await hearing from you with the proceeds of the account.

Yours faithfully

8.   Authority for Receiving Money

Any date

Bank plc
Address

Dear Sirs

Re   Name   –   deceased
**   Address**
**   Account No: Sort   Code:**
**   Account No: Sort Code:**

We hereby give you authority to let .... of
.... have the proceeds due to the Estate of the
Late ....
Signature   ....
                         Name:

Signature   ....
                         Name:

Dated   ....

9. Letter to Registrar to Transfer Shares

Any date

Registrars
Address

Dear Sirs

Re   Name   -   deceased
      .... Shares

We take this opportunity of enclosing the following:

1. Original Share Certificate

2. Stock Transfer Form duly signed by the Executors of the Estate

3. Office Copy Probate – Please return as soon as possible

We would be obliged if the Shares could be transferred into the name of ....

Kindly confirm to us when this has been completed.

Yours faithfully

10. Letter paying bills from the Estate

Any date

Address

Dear Sirs

Re   *Name*   –   deceased
Account Ref:

We take this opportunity of enclosing your account together with a cheque in the sum of £..............

Kindly return your account duly receipted in due course and we would be obliged if you would kindly confirm that there are no further outstanding sums and this account is clear.

Yours faithfully

11. Letter to Beneficiary with Statement for Approval

Any date
Beneficiary Name
Address

Dear ....

Re   *Name* – deceased

I take this opportunity of enclosing my statement of account. You will note that there is a retention of £............ which I will hold until I have confirmation that there are no further amounts due from the Estate.

If you would kindly confirm that the statement is in order I will arrange for your share of the residuary Estate to be paid to you immediately.

Yours sincerely

12. Letter Sending Pecuniary Legacy

Any dateAddress

Dear ....

Re *Name* **– deceased**
  Address:

We act for the Estate of .... deceased. *Name of deceased* left you a legacy of £........... and we have pleasure in enclosing a cheque for that amount together with a receipt which please sign, date and return to me

Yours sincerely

13.　Receipt for Pecuniary Legacy *(on behalf of ....)*

IN THE ESTATE OF .... - DECEASED

I .... the Treasurer of ....,
Address acknowledge to have received from the Executors of
Name deceased the sum of .... Thousand .... Hundred and
.... Pounds (£.........) being the pecuniary legacy bequeathed
to the .... by his / her Will.

Dated   Any date

Signed ....

14.   Receipt for Pecuniary Legacy

IN THE ESTATE OF .... - DECEASED

I .... acknowledge to have received from the Executors of .... deceased the sum of .... Thousand .... Hundred and .... Pounds and (£...............) being the pecuniary legacy bequeathed to me by his / her Will.

Dated   Any date

Signed ....

15. Letter to Beneficiary

Any date

Address

Dear ....

Re *Name* **– deceased**

I take this opportunity of enclosing a cheque in the sum of £.......... which is the amount due to you as one of the beneficiaries of the Estate. *I am holding a small retention of £........ for ....*

I also enclose a copy of the statement for your information and a receipt which please sign, date and return to me

Yours sincerely

16. Receipt for Beneficiary

IN THE ESTATE OF .... - DECEASED

I .... acknowledge to have received from the Executors   of .... deceased the sum of .... Pounds and .... Pence (£................) being the share of the residuary Estate bequeathed to me by his / her Will.

Dated   Any date

Signed ....

17. Instruction Sheet for a Will

Full Name: ....

Address: ....

....

Telephone No: ....

Executors: ....

Addresses: ....

Alternative Executors: ....

Addresses: ....

Beneficiaries: ....

....

Addresses: ....

....

(If the Beneficiaries are currently older than you, you may give consideration to appointing an alternative Beneficiary)

Alternative Beneficiaries: ....

Addresses ....

Any Specific Item you wish to give away: ....

....

Any Specific Sums of Money you wish to give away: ....

....

....

Any other wishes you may have (such as either being buried
or cremated)

....

....

Signed: ....

Dated: ....

****

GLOSSARY OF TERMS

A

Abatement -When the Estate has insufficient money to pay the bills, then any gifts will be reduced pro rata to make enough money to pay such bills, debts and expenses.

Ademption-If when the Will comes into effect, that is the date of the death, the gift does not exist, the gift lapses. It may have been sold or given away during the deceased's lifetime.

Administrator/Administrix-In the event of an Intestacy, this is a definition of a person who deals with the deceased's estate.

Assent-A document which transfer the freehold or leasehold property to the beneficiary.

Assets-Everything belonging to the deceased

Attestation Clause-A note at the end of the Will, confirming that the Will has been properly signed and witnessed.

B

Bankruptcy-When a person cannot pay their debts, they can apply to the Court to have themselves made bankrupt or you can make someone else bankrupt if you are a creditor. The bankrupts' affairs are then run by the Trustee in bankruptcy until they are discharged.

Beneficiary-beneficiary of a will

Bequeathed-Old fashioned word meaning – To leave someone property, more likely now to be bequest. A gift other than cash can be money or shares or other physical items.

Bona Vacantia-In the event of no other relative being alive, there is no one to inherit it goes to the Crown

C

Capacity-This means both mental and being of age that is 18 years old to be able to act as Executor or Administrator and a Beneficiary needs capacity to be able to receive the gift and give a valid receipt.

Capital Gains Tax (CGT)-When an asset has been owned during the deceased's lifetime and is sold for more than it was acquired for, then after deduction of allowances and reliefs, this tax is payable.

Caveat-A caution which will be given to the Probate Registry when there is doubt about the validity of the Will or whether there is a dispute about who is entitled to be the Executor.

Chargeable Gift-Anything left under the terms of the Will or during a person's lifetime, which is liable to tax.

Chattels-These are such things as pets, cars, boats, furniture, jewellery ornaments etc.   Business assets money and securities are not chattels.

Children-The covers both legitimate and illegitimate children together with legally adopted children. This does not include stepchildren.

Codicil-An additional Will to make changes in your original Will.

Contentious Probate-Where someone lodges a caveat preventing the issue of a grant and their objections over such matters as the validity of the Will or the entitlement of someone to apply for the grant.

Continent Gift-Something left with a condition attached, which is an age or a condition.

Conveyancing-The process by which land and buildings are transferred.

Court of Protection-Any Power of Attorney either registered or unregistered or the persons affairs were with the Receivers then all such powers lapse on death.

D

Death Certificate-When a death is registered you should obtain extra copies for anyone who needs them. Most institutions want to see the original copy, not a photocopy.

Devise-Old fashioned word meaning to give

Deeds of Variation-If all the beneficiaries agree, then after the death, the terms of the Will may be altered, usually for the purpose of saving Inheritance Tax. It has to be drawn up within two years of the date of death.

Distribution of the Estate-Once probate has been granted, and all monies have been collected it, all debts and taxes have been paid and the accounts agreed, then the Estate may be distributed.

Donation of Organs-The deceased may give directions for the disposal of their body. The decision is that of the Executors who will generally follow the wishes of the deceased

E

Enduring Power of Attorney (EPOA)-If an Enduring Power of Attorney was being used prior to death this will cease on death.

Engrossment-A final copy of a document.

Excepted Estate-These are estates under a certain limit that do not have to be notified to the Inland Revenue

Executor/Executrix-The Person named in the Will to deal with the deceased Estate.

G

Grant of Letter of Administration-This means the dealing with the deceased's Estate after death. The administration is undertaken by an Administrator, if there is no Will or an Executor if there is a Will.

Grant of Probate-This is where there is a Will and an Executor has been appointed.

Guardians-People appointed by the Will, another parent or the Court to act with parental responsibility for a child.

H

Half Blood-Where people share only one parent in common, they are of the half blood. For example Brother of the half blood.

Headstones-Reasonable costs of the headstone can be deducted with the funeral from the Estate together with reasonable cost of the wake. Again, depending on the size of the Estate.

I

IHT-Inheritance Tax

Intestacy-Where no Will has been made

Intestate-The person who Dies without making a Will

Issue-Or living descendant

J

Joint Tenant-Usually the surviving spouse and the property automatically passes to the surviving spouse and there is an Inheritance Tax exemption.

Joint Assets-Two or more persons have a legal interest in a property, usually land and buildings. Normally, all the other joint owners inherit automatically. They are assessed for Inheritance Tax purposes, even though they pass automatically to the surviving joint owners. A proper valuation should be made.

L

Land Registry-Land Registry www.landreg.gov.uk.

Leasehold property-The Executor/Administrator retains any rights that the original Leaseholder would have had, such as being able to buy the freehold etc.

Legacy-A gift left to someone in a Will other than house or land.

Letter of Administration-Equivalent to the Grant of Probate where no Will has been made

Liabilities-Another word for debts. They need to be identified and show in any probate application. Any creditors will need to be informed and once funds have been gathered these debts should be paid off.

Life Interest-The right to enjoy the benefit for life.

M

Minor/Infant-Any child under the age of 18

N

Newspaper Advertisements-These involve Obituary Notices and Trustee Act Notices

O

Oath-An oath is a sworn statement, usually whilst holding the Bible but an affirmation of the truth can be made instead of swearing on the Bible.

Office Copy Entries-This is evidence of the property title at the Land Registry.

P

Pecuniary Legacy-Any Specific amount of money

Personal Representative-Can mean either the Executor or Administrator, just a general term to cover them both.

Probate-Confirmation that the Will is valid and the Executors have the authority to deal with the Estate

R

Renunciation-The Executor has the right to renounce, which means giving up his or her right to be the Executor. To renounce the Executor needs to sign a Form or Letter of Renunciation, which is then sent to the Probate Registry by the proving Executor

Residue-This is the Estate of the deceased, which remains after distribution to the beneficiaries after payment of all gifts and all taxes, debts etc.

Revocation of Will-This means to cancel any previously written Will. Usually a new Will will revoke a previously written Will or it can be revoked in other ways by destroying it etc.

S

Small Estate-Any Estate under the figure of £5000.00

Specific Legacy-A gift of some specific item such as a physical item – car or an amount of money

Spouse-Old legal term for a Wife or Husband.

Survivorship-Where two or more joint Tenants have outlived the deceased. The joint Tenant then inherits a share of the Estate automatically by survivorship. No probate needs to be proved.

T

Tenant-Either a joint tenant or tenant in common. Confusing to the public as this is nothing to do with leasehold property. Therefore you can be a joint tenant or tenant in common of freehold property.

Tenants in common-This is where property is held by two or more people in different shares. Unless shown otherwise, it will usually be fifty/fifty like joint tenants. If one Tenant dies their share passes according to the Will.

Testamentary expenses-Reasonable costs incurred in the administration of the estate. Professional Executors are unable to receive compensation unless it is specific term of the Will.

Testator/Testatrix-This is a person making the Will. Testatrix is the female form.

Trust-An arrangement to hold property for another. The Trustee is not the legal owner.

Trustees-This is where somebody who is responsible to hold Trust assets on behalf of the beneficiaries.

U

Unregistered Land-Certain areas of land have not been registered as there has been no transfer or other variation of the Title. This is equally as affective as registered land but the Land Registry are changing the rules so within the foreseeable future, all land will become registered.

Undue Influence-Where pressure either mental or physical will be put on a party to do an act against their will.

Validity of Will-For a Will to be valid it has to be in writing, signed, witnessed correctly and the Testator has to know he or she is signing.

W

Will-A formal document outlining who is to be your executor after death and to whom you leave possessions etc.

****

Useful Addresses

Department for National Savings

Glasgow G58 1SB
For enquiries about Capital Bonds, Childrens Bonus Bonds, FIRST Option Bonds, Fixed Rate Savings Bonds, Ordinary Accounts and Investment Accounts.
www.nsandi.com
Tel: 08085 007 007

Department of Work and Pensions
Caxton House
Tothill Street
London
SW1H 9NA
www.dwpguide.co.uk

HM Revenue and Customs Capital Taxes Office
Tel: 0300 200 3300

The Law Society of England and Wales
www.lawsociety.org.uk

London Gazette
PO Box 3548
Norwich NR7 7WD
0333 200 2434 www.thegazette.co.uk

Solicitors Regulation Authority
The Cube
199 Wharfside Street
Birmingham
B1 1RN
www.sra.org.uk
0370 606 2555
Information on solicitors specialising in wills and probate

The Principal Probate Registry
First Avenue House
42-49 High Holborn
London WC1V 6NP
Probate Helpline 0300 123 1072
Enquiries 0207 421 8509

Useful Addresses in Scotland
Accountant of Court
2 Parliament Square
Edinburgh EH1 1RQ
0131 240 6742
www.scotscourts.gov.uk

Law Society of Scotland

Atria One 144 Morrison Street
Edinburgh
EH3 8EX
0131 226 7411 www.lawscot.org.uk

Registers of Scotland

Customer Service Centre

Meadowbank House

153 London Road

Edinburgh

HE8 7AU

0800 169 9391

(Head Office)

Or

Registers of Scotland

Hanover House

24 Douglas Street

Glasgow

G2 7NQ

0800 169 9291

www.ros.gov.uk

Sheriff Clerks Office

Commissary Department

27 Chambers Street

Edinburgh EH1 1LB

0131 225 2525

****

Index

Schedule of Probate Forms

1. IHT205 – Return of Estate Information
2. IHT400 – Inland Revenue Account for Inheritance Tax
3. IHTWS – Inheritance Tax work sheet
4. Oath for Executors
5. Oath for Administrators
6. Stock / Share Transfer Form
7. AS1

The Following Probate Forms, which are shown overleaf, are obtainable on the website:

https://hmctsformfinder.justice.gov.uk

8. N205D – Notice of issue (Probate Claim)
9. PA1 - How to obtain Probate
10. PA1A - Guidance notes for Probate Application
11. PA1S- Application for Probate Search
12. PA2 -How to obtain Probate

    guide for the applicant without solicitor

14.PA4 - Directory of Probate Registries and

    interview venues

****

Notice of issue
(probate claim)

In the

Claim No.

Claimant(s)

Defendant(s)

Issue fee

In the estate of   deceased (Probate)

Your claim was issued on [   ]

[The court sent it to the defendant(s) by first class post on [   ]

and it will be deemed served on [   ]].

[The claim form (which includes particulars of claim) is returned to you, with the relevant response forms, for

you to serve them on the defendant(s)]

Notes for guidance
The claim form and particulars of claim, if served separately, must be served on the defendant within 4 months
of the date of issue (6 months if you are serving outside England and Wales). You may be able to apply to
extend the time for serving the claim form but the application must generally be made before the 4 month or
6 month period expires.

You must inform the court immediately if your claim is settled.

The defendant must file an acknowledgment of service and defence within 28 days of service of the Particulars
of Claim (whether they are served with the claim form or separately). A longer period applies if the defendant
is served outside England and Wales.

Default judgment **cannot** be obtained in a probate claim.

If no defendant acknowledges service or files a defence, and the time for doing so has expired, you may apply to
the court for an order that the claim proceed to trial.

To

Ref.

PA1— Probate application

When someone dies, you may need to get a Grant of Representation (known as 'probate'), a document that gives you the legal right to deal with their property, bank accounts, money and other possessions (their 'estate').

Leaflet **PA2** *How to obtain probate – A guide for people acting without a solicitor* explains this process. Further guidance is available online at www.gov.uk/wills-probate-inheritance. If you would like assistance, please telephone the **Probate Helpline** on 0300 123 1072. Probate staff can advise you about processes, but cannot provide you with legal advice.

Please complete this form using BLOCK CAPITALS, placing a tick ☑ in boxes where applicable. If you need more space for answers, please attach extra sheets of paper to your application.

1. Swearing the oath

You are required to swear an oath to state that information you provide in this application is true to the best of your knowledge and belief. Where would you like to do this?

☐ At a solicitor's office

☐ At a Probate Office, at the following District Probate Registry:

Note 1 – we will send you guidance about swearing the oath once you send us the completed application.

A list of District Probate Registries is available in leaflet **PA4**, which you can download from **hmctsformfinder.justice. gov.uk**

2. The person who has died

2.1 Forename(s) (including all middle names) as they appear on the Death Certificate

2.2 Surname as it appears on the Death Certificate

2.3 Permanent address

Postcode

2.4 Date they were born

2.5 Date they died

2.6 Did the person who has died hold any assets in another name?

☐ Yes, **go to question 2.7**

☐ No, **go to question 2.8**

2.7 Please give the details of any other names by which the person who has died held assets.

Full name

Note 2.7 – These names must be ones that will appear on the grant because an asset is in that name. We do not need to know the asset.

2.8 Did the person who died live permanently in England and Wales at the date of death, or intend to return to England and Wales to live permanently?

☐ Yes

☐ No

2.9 Was the person who has died legally adopted?

☐ Yes

☐ No

2.10 Was any relative of the person who has died legally adopted?

☐ Yes

☐ No, **go to question 2.12**

2.11 Please name the legally adopted relatives and give their relationship to the person who has died. Please state whether they were adopted into the family of the person who has died, or 'adopted out' (became part of someone else's family).

Name	Relationship	Adopted in or out

Note 2.8 – Living permanently means they had a lasting connection with England and Wales such as having been born in England and Wales and retaining a home there. They may have lived abroad but planned to return to England and Wales to live permanently. For legal purposes this means they were domiciled in England and Wales. You may wish to seek legal advice about this.

Note 2.9 – the names of legally adopted people are entered in the Adopted Children's Register. If your relationship with the person who has died was through adoption (e.g. they adopted you, or you adopted them) and they did not leave a will, please obtain a copy of their entry in the Register from The General Register Office, Adoptions Section, Trafalgar Road, Birkdale, Southport PR8 2HH and provide it with your form.

2.12 What was the marital status of the person who has died when they died?

☐ Never married, **go to section 3**

☐ Widowed, their spouse or civil partner having died before them, **go to section 3**

☐ Married/in a civil partnership, **go to section 3**

☐ Divorced/civil partnership is dissolved – If the person who has died made a will go to section 3 or if they did not leave a will go to question 2.13.

☐ Judicially separated – If the person who has died made a will go to section 3 or if they did not leave a will go to question 2.13.

2.13 What is the name of their former spouse or civil partner?

[   ]

2.14 What was the date of their divorce, dissolution or judicial separation?

[| | | | |]

2.15 What is the name of the court where the Decree Absolute, Decree of Dissolution of Partnership or Decree of Judicial Separation was issued?

[   ]

Note 2.12 – a civil partnership is a same-sex relationship that has been registered in accordance with the Civil Partnership Act 2004.

Note 2.14 – this date is on their Decree Absolute, Decree of Dissolution of Partnership or Decree of Judicial Separation. You can get an official copy of these documents from the court that issued them, or from The Divorce Absolute Search Section, Central Family Court, 42–49 High Holborn, London WC1V 6NP.

3. The will and any codicils

3.1 Did the person who has died leave a will?

☐ Yes, **please provide the original document(s) with your application**

☐ No, **go to section 4**

3.2 Did the person who has died leave any codicils?

☐ Yes, **please provide the original codicil document(s) with your application**

☐ No

3.3 Is the will dated **before** 4 April 1988?

☐ Yes

☐ No

3.4 Did the person who has died marry or enter into a civil partnership **after** the date of the will or any codicils?

☐ Yes, please give the date of the marriage or civil partnership

☐ No

3.5 Is there anyone under 18 years old who receives a gift in the will or a codicil?

☐ Yes

☐ No

3.6 Do any of the witnesses to the signing of the will, their spouses or their civil partners receive a gift under the will or a codicil?

☐ Yes

☐ No

3.7 Name any executors who are **not** making this application with you, and explain why.

Reasons for executors not applying:

A – They died before the person who has died.

B – They died after the person who has died.

C – Power reserved: they have chosen not to apply, but reserve the right to do so later.

D – Renunciation: they have chosen not to apply, and give up all rights to apply.

E – Power of attorney: they will appoint another person to act as their attorney to take a Grant of Representation on their behalf

Full name(s) of executor(s) **not** applying	A, B, C, D or E

3.8 ☐ I/we declare that I/we have given written notice to all executors who have power reserved to them and are not making this application.

Note 3.1 – a will does not have to be a formal document. Please make sure you send the original will with your application. If you do not then this will delay your application.

Note 3.2 – a codicil is a document that amends a will.

Note 3.7 – we need to know why any executors aren't included in this application. This includes any executors who have pre-deceased.

Reason C – If any executors are having power reserved, you **must** notify them of the application in writing. The Grant of Representation will only be issued to those people named as applicants in section 6.

The attorney of one executor and an executor acting in their own right may not jointly apply for a Grant of Representation.

Reason D – if you state that an executor has given up their right to apply, when we receive this application we will send another form to you to give to the executor, for them to sign.

Note – if you fail to give written notice, it is likely to delay your application.

4. Foreign domicile

Note – if you answered Yes, to question 2.8 you don't need to complete this section – please go to **section 5**.

4.1 What was the country where the person who died either lived permanently at the date of death or intended to return to live permanently?

4.2 What does the estate in England and Wales of the person has died consist of?

Assets	Values

4.3 Did the person who has died have any wills that were made outside of England and Wales?

☐ Yes, **please provide an official copy with your application; if it is not in English, please also provide a translation**

☐ No

4.4 Did the person who has died own any foreign assets?

☐ Yes, the total value of their foreign assets (not including houses or land):

£

☐ No

4.5 Has an entrusting document, a succession certificate or an inheritance certificate been issued in the country of domicile of the person who has died?

☐ Yes, **please provide the document with your application; if it is not in English, please also provide a translation**

☐ No

Note 4.5 – these documents may help to support your application. If you do not have any of these documents, you may wish to seek legal advice.

5. Relatives of the person who has died

5.1 Did the person who has died leave a surviving spouse or civil partner?

☐ Yes, **complete question 5.2**

☐ No, **complete questions 5.2 and 5.3**

Note 5.1 – 'survive' means that they were alive when the deceased person died.

5.2 How many of the following blood and adoptive relatives did person who has died have?

	Under 18 years	Over 18 year
5.2a Sons or daughters who survived them		
5.2b Sons or daughters who did not survive them		
5.2c Children of people at 5.2b who survived them		
5.2d Parents who survived them		
5.2e Whole-blood brothers or sisters who survived them		
5.2f Whole-blood brothers or sisters who did not survive them		
5.2g Children of people at 5.2f who survived them		
5.2h Half-blood brothers or sisters who survived them		
5.2i Half-blood brothers or sisters who did not survive them		
5.2j Children of people at 5.2i who survived them		

Note 5.2 – Sections a, b, and c should be completed for all applications. Please state the **number** of relatives the person who has died had in the relevant sections. If none then put nil or strike through. If your answer to question 5.1 is no, once you have entered a number of surviving relatives in one of the block sections (e.g. 5.2a-5.2c) please move on to question 6.

Step-relatives should not be included.

A '**whole-blood**' brother or sister is someone who has both parents in common with person who has died, or someone who was legally adopted by both of the parents of the person who has died.

A '**half-blood**' brother or sister is someone who has only one parent in common with the person who has died, or someone who was legally adopted by only one of the parents of the person who has died.

5.3 How many of the following blood and adoptive relatives did the person who has died have?

	Under 18 years	Over 18 year
5.3a Grandparents who survived them		
5.3b Whole-blood uncles or aunts who survived them		
5.3c Whole-blood uncles or aunts who did not survive them		
5.3d Children of people at 5.3c who survived them		
5.3e Half-blood uncles or aunts who survived them		
5.3f Half-blood uncles or aunts who did not survive them		
5.3g Children of people at 5.3f who survived them		

Note 5.3 – This section should only be completed if no relatives have been entered in section 5.2. Please state the **number** of relatives the person who has died had in the relevant sections. If none then put nil or strike through. Once you have entered a number in one of the block sections (e.g. 5.3b–5.3d) please move on to question 6.

Step-relatives and people who were related to the person who has died only by marriage should not be included.

A '**whole-blood**' uncle or aunt is someone who has both parents in common with the mother or father of person who has died, or someone who was legally adopted by the maternal or paternal grandparents of the person who has died .

A '**half-blood**' uncle or aunt is someone who has only one parent in common with the mother or father of the person who has died or someone who was legally adopted by only one of the grandparents of the person who has died.

6. About the applicant(s)

6.1 Title and full name including middle names of **first applicant**

6.2 Your address

Postcode

6.3 Your home telephone number

6.4 Your mobile/work telephone number

6.5 Your email address

6.6 Your relationship to the person who has died

6.7 Title and full name including middle names of **second applicant**

6.8 Their address

Postcode

6.9 Their relationship to the person who has died

Note 6 – all correspondence, including the Grant of Representation, will be sent to the first applicant named in this section.

Only list applicants who wish to be named on the grant in this section as they will be required to swear the oath.

Note 6.5 – we will contact you with any queries via this email address. We will also send you your oath via this email account. We aim to contact you within 10 working days of receipt of your application.

6.10 Title and full name including middle names of **third applicant**

6.11 Their address

Postcode

6.12 Their relationship to the person who has died

6.13 Title and full name including middle names of **fourth applicant**

6.14 Their address

Postcode

6.15 Their relationship to the person who has died

7.   Inheritance tax

7.1   Did you complete an Inheritance Tax Estate report online?

☐   Yes, do not submit an Inheritance Tax form with this application

Please provide the following details, **then go to section 8**:

IHT Identifier

Gross Estate Figure   £

Net Estate Figure   £

☐   No, **go to question 7.2**

7.2   Which of the following inheritance tax forms have you completed?

☐   Form **IHT205**, **complete 7.3 then go to section 8**

☐   Form **IHT207**, **complete 7.4 then go to section 8**

☐   Forms **IHT400** and **IHT421**, **complete 7.5 then go to section 8**

Note 7.2 – if you did not complete an Inheritance Tax Estate report online, you **must** complete IHT205, or IHT207, or both IHT400 and IHT421.

7.3   Provide the following figures from form **IHT205**.

Figure from box D   £

Figure from box F   £
(This figure will determine the probate application fee (See PA3))

Note 7.3 – if the person who has died, died before 1st September 2006, it may affect which tax form you need to complete, so please ring the **Probate Helpline** on **0300 123 1072**.

7.4   Provide the following figures from form **IHT207**.

Figure from box A   £

Figure from box H   £
(This figure will determine the probate application fee (See PA3))

7.5   Provide the following figures from form **IHT421**.

Figure from box 3   £
(Gross value of assets)

Figure from box 5   £
(Net value)
(This figure will determine the probate application fee (See PA3))

Note 7.5 – do **not** send form IHT400 or form IHT421 to us. Please send them to HM Revenue and Customs, Inheritance Tax, BX9 1HT, at the same time you send PA1 and other papers to the District Probate Registry. HMRC will stamp your IHT421 and send it to the District Probate Registry you named on your IHT421.

8. Applying as an attorney

8.1 Are you applying as an attorney on behalf of one or more people who are entitled to apply for a Grant of Representation?

☐ Yes

☐ No, **go to section 9**

Note 8 – if you are applying on behalf of more than one person, please provide the information requested in this section for the other people you represent on a separate sheet of paper.

8.2 Please give the full names of the person or people on whose behalf you are applying.

8.3 Please give their address

Postcode

8.4 In what capacity are they entitled to apply?

Note 8.4 – for example, as an executor named in the will, or on the basis of their relationship to the person who has died if there is no will.

8.5 Is a person on whose behalf you are applying unable to make a decision for themselves due to an impairment of or a disturbance in the functioning of their mind or brain?

☐ Yes, further confirmation of this will be requested by the Probate Registry.

☐ No

Note 8.5 – this applies if they lack capacity under the Mental Capacity Act 2005 and are incapable of managing their property and financial affairs. You may wish to seek legal advice about this.

8.6 Has anyone been appointed by the Court of Protection to act on behalf of a person on whose behalf you are applying?

☐ Yes, **please provide an official copy of the court order with your application**

☐ No

8.7 Has a person on whose behalf you are applying appointed an attorney under an Enduring Power of Attorney (EPA) or a Property and Financial Affairs Lasting Power of Attorney (LPA)?

☐ Yes, **please provide the original EPA/LPA (or a solicitor's certified copy of it) with your application**

☐ No, **go to section 9**

Note 8.7 – an LPA must be registered with the Office of the Public Guardian before it can be used.

8.8 Has the Enduring Power of Attorney (EPA) been registered with the Office of the Public Guardian?

☐ Yes

☐ No

9. Checklist

Please send this application to one of the main Probate Registries (see leaflet PA4). Before you submit your application form, please complete this checklist to confirm that you have enclosed the relevant documents and fees, and if applicable tick the declaration.

- [ ] PA1 (Probate Application Form)
- [ ] Inheritance Tax Summary Form: Please submit the appropriate form (IHT205 or IHT207, and IHT217 if applicable), signed by all applicants.
- [ ] The original will and any codicils, plus three plain (not certified) unstapled A4-sized copies of the will and any codicils.
- [ ] An official copy of any foreign wills or any wills dealing with assets held outside England and Wales (and if not in English, an English translation).
- [ ] An official copy (**not** a photocopy) of the death certificate, or a coroner's interim certificate of the person who has died.
- [ ] Any other documents requested on this form. Please list them:

- [ ] A cheque/postal order payable to '**HMCTS**' in respect of HMCTS's fees. Please write the name of the person who has died on the back of the cheque/postal order. As well as the application fee, there is a fee for each official copy of the Grant of Representation that we provide (see the fee list leaflet **PA3**).

How many official copies of the Grant of Representation do you require for use **in** England and Wales?

How many official copies of the Grant of Representation do you require for use **outside** of England and Wales?

Application fee	£
Fees for copies	£
Total fees	£

Please note: Only the main probate registries (as shown on form PA4) can receive applications and fees, no other probate registries can accept applications or take any form of payment.

Note 9 – if you completed an Inheritance Tax Summary online, **and** fully complete question 7.1 of this form, you do not need to send an Inheritance Tax Estate report form with your application.

Do not attach anything to or remove anything from the original will/codicils. If you separated the original will for photocopying, please explain this in a covering letter. Also, make sure that you keep a copy for yourself.

If you do not enclose all of the required documents, it will take us longer to process your application. Please ensure that the information that you provide is accurate, and keep copies of all documents.

If you have declared assets in a foreign country on the tax return it may be necessary to order copies of the grant for use outside England and Wales, please check with the asset holder.

Also, if the person who has died was domiciled in England and Wales the grant of representation we issue will cover the whole of the UK i.e. England, Wales, Scotland and Northern Ireland.

Guidance Notes
for Probate Application Form PA1

These notes will help you to complete the parts of form PA1 marked *

Section A

A1 Please enclose the original will and any codicils with your application (**not** a photocopy).

A6 Please state the names of any executors named in the will who are not applying for the Grant of Probate and show one of the following reasons for this:-

A The executor died before the deceased.

B The executor died after the deceased.

C The executor does not wish to apply for probate now but wishes to reserve the right to act as executor in the future if necessary – this option is referred to as having "power reserved".

D The executor does not wish to apply for probate at all. This is referred to as "renouncing". It means that they gives up all their rights to act as executor.

E The executor wants to appoint another person to act as their attorney to take the Grant of Representation out on their behalf. Please note, however, that the attorney of one executor cannot take a grant jointly with an executor acting in his own right.

If you give reason D or E, please send a letter signed by the executor stating their intention when you send the application to the Probate Registry. If option C, D, or E is stated the Probate Registry will, on receipt of your application, send you a form for the executor(s) to sign to confirm their intention. You should arrange for this to be completed and then return it to the Probate Registry as instructed.

Example for A6

A will appoints three executors – Brian Jones, Valerie Jones and Frank Smith. Brian Jones wishes to apply for the grant, Frank Smith dies before the deceased and Valerie Jones does not wish to apply for the grant at present, as she works full time and cannot attend the appointment. Valerie wishes to keep her options open however, just in case it becomes necessary for her to take out a Grant of Probate in future e.g. if Brian Jones dies before he has completed the administration. The form would be completed as follows:

Frank Smith	A
Valerie Jones	C

The Grant of Probate will issue to Brian Jones with "power reserved" to Valerie Jones. Valerie Jones will be asked to sign a "power reserved" form.

Section B

Sections B1 - B4 must be completed in all cases. Sections B5 - B6 only needs to be completed if the deceased had no relatives in Sections B1 - B4.

Note:

- This section refers to blood/legally adopted relatives only; details of step relatives are not required.
- The term "survived" means the person was alive when the deceased died.
- If the deceased had any half brothers or sisters/uncles/aunts (i.e. only one parent in common), please indicate this on the form.
- A civil partnership is defined as one between two people of the same sex which has been registered in accordance with the Civil Partnership Act 2004.

B2(c), B4(c) and B6(c)

B2(c) – Only include children of sons or daughters of the deceased entered in B2(b), where the children have survived the deceased.

B4(c) – Only include children of brothers or sisters of the deceased entered in B4(b), where the children have survived the deceased.

B6(c) – Only include children of uncles or aunts of the deceased entered in B6(b), where the children have survived the deceased.

© Crown Copyright 2008

Section C

If you are applying on behalf of the person entitled to the grant (i.e. as their attorney), you should send a letter signed by them confirming that they want you to apply with your application. If the person entitled to the grant has already signed an Enduring Power of Attorney (EPA), or a Property and financial affairs Lasting Power of Attorney (LPA) please send the original document to us. An LPA must be registered with the Office of the Public Guardian before it can be used. If the donor of the EPA or LPA is unable to make a decision for him/herself due to an impairment of or a disturbance in the functioning of the mind or brain (i.e. lacks capacity under the Mental Capacity Act (MCA) 2005) please contact us.

Section D

D1 - D2 Please state the full **true** name of the deceased. The true name usually consists of the forenames as shown on the person's birth certificate and the surname as shown on the death certificate. If this is not the case please contact us.

D3 - D4 If the deceased had any assets in any name(s) other than their true name these should be stated. You do not need to show here any assets held jointly with another person.

Example for D1 - D4:

Name on birth certificate	Emma Louise **Jones**
Name on death certificate	Emma Louise **Smith**

The deceased's true name is Emma Louise Smith.

The deceased had a bank account in the name of Louise Smith and was commonly known by this name. The form should be completed as follows:

Forenames	**Emma Louise**
Surname	Smith
Did the deceased hold any assets (excluding joint assets) in another name?	Yes
If yes, what are the assets?	Lloyds Bank Account
And in what name(s) are they held?	**Louise** Smith

The grant will issue in the name of "Emma Louise Smith otherwise known as Louise Smith".

D8 The domicile of the deceased at the date of their death must be established in each case. Generally a person is domiciled in the country which they consider to be their permanent home. However they may be domiciled in a country without having a permanent home there. If you are unsure what this means you should contact your local registry. You may need to seek legal advice regarding this.

D9 You do not initially need to supply a copy of the Decree Absolute, decree of dissolution of civil partnership or decree of Judicial Separation if the deceased left a will. However we may ask to see it later if necessary. You can obtain an official copy of these documents from the court that issued them or from Principal Registry of the Family Division, 42-49 High Holborn, London WC1V 6NP.

D10 - D11 If the deceased did **not** leave a will and the applicant for the grant is the adoptor/adoptee of the deceased, please file a copy of the entry in the Adopted Children's Register. An official copy of the entry in the Adopted Children's Register can be obtained from The General Register Office, Adoption Section, Smedley Hydro, Trafalgar Road, Birkdale, Southport PR8 2HH.

**If you have any general enquiries,
please telephone the Probate and Inheritance Tax Helpline
Telephone number: 0300 123 1072**

Application for a probate search (copies of grants and wills)

When completing your form please use CAPITAL LETTERS   www.justice.gov.uk

Details of the Deceased

Surname

Forenames

Alternative spellings   Forenames: Surname:

Probate details (if known)   Grant type: Issuing Registry: Grant issue date:

Date of death   Search period

Please note we search up to 4 years as part of the fee but if you want us to search a wider period the charge is £4 for every 4-year period (see notes on next page).

Address

Document requirements/payment

Do you want a copy of the Will (if any)?   Yes ☐   No ☐   If Yes, how many? ☐

Do you want a copy of the Grant of Probate   Yes ☐   No ☐   If Yes, how many? ☐
or Letters of Administration (if any)?

I am the administrator/executor of the estate   ☐ (tick if appropriate)

I enclose a crossed cheque/Postal Order   (see notes on fees
(payable to HM Courts & Tribunals Service) to the value of: £   on next page)

Your own details

Name/Organisation

Your ref. (if any)

Address/DX number and
Exchange

Please send the completed form, together with your payment, by post to: The Postal Searches and Copies Department, Leeds District Probate Registry, York House, York Place, Leeds LS1 2BA

For official use

Postal Searches and Copies Department: Information and Conditions of Service

Applicable dates and records held: The Postal Searches and Copies Department has access to indexes relating to all Probate records for the whole of England and Wales from 11 January 1858 up to the present day. You may apply for a copy of any proved Will, as well as a copy of the Grant of Representation. The Grant will tell you who were the Executors or Administrators (those appointed to gather in and distribute the estate). It may also tell you the name of the Solicitor acting for them (if any) and the value of the estate, although usually only in very broad terms. The financial summary shown on the Grant is the only information relating to the estate that the Probate record contains. No inventory or estate accounts are available. Occasionally, further details are available from the Capital Taxes Office, but you will normally need the written consent of the executors or administrators. **Please note that, if Probate has not been granted, the Probate Service will have no record of the estate and will therefore not be able to provide copies of any document relating to it. Please also note that sealed copies are only available to executors/administrators of an estate.**

If the death was recent, it may be that Probate has not yet been cleared. Consequently, it may be advisable to wait two or three months after the date of death before having a search made, in order to allow time for the Probate process to be completed.

If you apply before Probate has been completed, you will be notified that no details are available. If you wish to pursue your enquiry, you will need to reapply after a suitable interval, enclosing a further fee and resubmitting all the relevant details, or enter a Standing Search. A Standing Search remains in force for a period of 6 months from the date of entry and provides copies of the Will (if any) and Grant if a Grant issues during this period. Contact any Probate Registry for further details.

Queries: If you have a query about an application you have submitted, please write to The Postal Searches and Copies Department, Leeds District Probate Registry, York House, York Place, Leeds LS1 2BA. It is not possible to telephone the Postal Searches and Copies Department and no other Probate Registry can answer queries about searches sent to that address.

Other parts of the UK and the Republic of Ireland: The jurisdiction of the Probate Service is limited to England and Wales. If the deceased died domiciled in Scotland, you could try contacting HM Commissary Office, 27 Chambers Street, Edinburgh EH1 2NS (Tel: 0131 247 2850) if the death occurred after 1985, or the Scottish Records Office, HM General Register House, Edinburgh EH1 3YY (Tel: 0131 535 1334) for records prior to this. For Northern Ireland, contact the Probate and Matrimonial Office, The Royal Courts of Justice, Belfast BT1 3JF (Tel: 028 9023 5111), or, if the death occurred more than 7 years ago, the Public Record Office of Northern Ireland, 66 Balmoral Street, Belfast, BT9 6NY (Tel: 028 9025 1318). For the Republic of Ireland, contact the Probate Office, Fourt Courts, Dublin 7 (Tel: Dublin 725555), or the National Archives Office, Bishop Street, Dublin 8 (Tel: Dublin 407 2300) for records more than 20 years old. The Channel Islands and the Isle of Man also have independent Probate Courts.

Fees: When returning the completed application to the Postal Searches and Copies Department in Leeds, please also enclose the fee of £6.00. Each **extra copy** of the same document ordered at the same time will attract an additional fee of £1.00. Cheques or Postal Orders should be crossed and made payable to 'HM Courts & Tribunals Service'. Fees from abroad should be paid by International Money Order, cheque or draft, payable through a United Kingdom bank, and must be made out in £ sterling. We are currently unable to accept payments by credit or debit card, nor are we able to receive search requests by telephone. Please contact any Probate Registry for details of fees for special copies (for instance if you are administering estate abroad), and mark your application accordingly.

The standard fee covers a 4-year search starting from the year in which the death occurred (or the year from which you ask us to start searching). Longer searches are charged at a rate of £4.00 per 4-year period, so that an 8-year search will cost £10.00, and a 12-year search £14.00. Please specify the period to be searched (as well as the date of death if known) and send the appropriate fee. If the death occurred within the last 4 years, the search will be made up to the most recent index. If the search is successful, we will obtain and forward copies of the Will and/or Grant as requested. If no Grant has issued in this time, you will be notified accordingly. We aim to respond to your request within 21 working days.

If a record is traced, the standard fee includes one copy of the Will, if any, and Grant, if requested. If the details you supply are incomplete, ambiguous or incorrect and the documents cannot be traced as a result, you will be asked to reapply, giving the correct information and enclosing a further payment. We cannot accept responsibility for the accuracy of the search unless full and correct details are given that accord with the information supplied on application for the Grant, normally the information in the Register of Deaths. If there is insufficient information to make a search, we will contact you for further details. **Please note that your payment is not refundable in the event of a negative search result.**

Copies or results of a negative search will be sent from the Probate Records Centre where our records are stored.

Original documents: If you are applying for copies of older documents, you should be aware that some of these are in poor condition. Although we make every effort to produce a legible copy from the documents we hold, a small proportion will be of unavoidable poor quality.

How to obtain probate -

A guide for people acting without a solicitor

What is the Probate Service?

The Probate Service is part of HM Courts & Tribunals Service. It administers the system of probate, which gives people the legal right to handle the estate (for example, money, possessions and property) of a deceased person.

This leaflet will advise you if you want to obtain probate without using a solicitor.

If you have any queries, please contact your local probate registry. The staff are there to help you – but please note that they cannot give you legal advice.

Introduction

When a person dies, they usually leave an estate (including money, possessions and property) and sometimes a will.

A will should name one or more executors who are responsible for collecting in all the money, paying any debts and distributing any legacies left to individuals or organisations.

In order to access the estate, the executor needs to apply to the probate registry for a document called a Grant of Representation or 'grant'. This process is called probate. The grant establishes who can legally collect money from banks, building societies and other organisations which hold assets belonging to the deceased person.

In most cases, applying for probate is a straightforward procedure. The Probate Service administers applications for grants throughout England and Wales.

The information in this leaflet refers only to the law in England and Wales. If the deceased person was permanently resident in Scotland, Northern Ireland or another country when they died, please contact your nearest probate registry for advice.

What is the purpose of the Grant of Representation?

A Grant of Representation establishes who can legally collect money from banks, building societies and other organisations that hold assets belonging to the deceased person. There are three types of Grant of Representation:

Probate

Probate is issued by the Probate Service to the executor(s) named in the deceased person's will.

Letters of Administration (with will)

Letters of Administration (with will) are issued when no executor is named in the will, or when the executors are unable or unwilling to apply for the grant.

Letters of Administration

Letters of Administration are issued when the deceased person has not made a will, or the will they have made is not valid.

Is a grant always needed?

Not every estate needs a grant. A grant may not be needed if:

- the home is held in joint names and is passing by survivorship to the other joint owner(s). This can be the case for married couples and those in a legal civil partnership.
- there is a joint bank or building society account. In this case, the bank may only need to see the death certificate, in order to arrange for the money to be transferred to the other joint owner. However, a grant could still be needed to access assets held in other bank accounts or insurance policies.
- the amount held in each account was very small. You will need to check with the organisations (banks, building societies or insurance companies) involved to find out if they will release the assets without a grant.

If none of the circumstances above apply, a grant may be required.

You should ask anyone holding the deceased's money (such as a bank or insurance company) whether they will release it to you without seeing a grant. If they agree, they may attach conditions such as asking you to sign a statutory declaration before a solicitor. You can decide whether it is cheaper or easier to do this than to apply for a grant.

Please note that a grant **must** be presented in order to sell or transfer a property held in the deceased's sole name or a share of a property held jointly with the deceased person's spouse or partner as tenants-in-common. Tenancy-in-common is a written agreement between two people who own a joint asset (usually land or buildings). Normally, a married couple does not have a tenancy-in-common contract. If you aren't sure about this, you should consult a solicitor.

You cannot complete a sale on any property owned by a deceased person until the grant has been issued. Properties named in a will should not be put up for sale until a grant has been obtained.

Who can apply for probate?

It isn't necessary for everyone left money or property in a will to apply for probate. Usually, only one person needs to do it – normally the executor(s) named in the will.

However, if the person entitled to the estate is under 18, two people are legally required to apply for probate. If this is the case we will let you know when we receive your application.

You can apply for probate if you are over the age of 18 and:

- you are an executor named in the will;
- you are named in the will to receive some or all of the estate (if there are no executors, or if the executors are unable or unwilling to apply);

- the deceased person did not make a will and you are their next of kin, in the following order of priority:

- lawful husband or wife or civil partner (a civil partnership is defined as a partnership between two people of the same sex which has been registered in accordance with the Civil Partnership Act 2004). Common law partners cannot apply for probate.

- sons or daughters (excluding step-children) including children adopted by the deceased. (Children adopted out of the family can only apply in the estates of their adoptive parents and not their biological parents.)

- parents

- brothers or sisters

- grandparents

- uncles or aunts

- If sons, daughters, brothers, sisters, uncles or aunts of the deceased person have died before the deceased, their children may apply for probate.

If you are not sure whether you are entitled to apply for a grant, you should still complete and return the forms and we will tell you. If you are a distant relative, please supply a brief family tree showing your relationship to the deceased person.

When more than one person wants to apply for a grant, they may make a joint application. A maximum of four applicants is allowed and they will all have to attend an interview with the Probate Service.

Where will I find the will?
The original will may be held at a solicitor's office or bank, or at the Principal Probate Registry in London. It may be among the deceased person's possessions. If you cannot find it, contact your local Probate Registry. If you do not send the will, your application will take longer to deal with.

We will not return the original will to you as it becomes a public record once it has been proved (acted on). We will, however, send you an official copy of the will with the Grant of Representation.

What if I don't want to apply for a grant?

Executors may choose to give up all their rights to probate or they may reserve the right, called power reserved, to apply for probate in the future.

This option is often used when the executors live in different parts of the country or it is not convenient for one of them to attend the interview due to work commitments.

Only the executor(s) who attend the interview will be named on the grant and only their signature will be required to release the deceased person's assets for transfer or sale.

If the person who is entitled to the grant does not wish to apply, they may appoint someone else to be their attorney to obtain the grant on their behalf. If this is the case you should complete their details on form **PA1** (Section C). We will send you a form for them to sign after we receive your application. If the person entitled to the grant has already signed an Enduring Power of Attorney (EPA) or a Lasting Power of Attorney (LPA) please file the original document with your application.

Note – A LPA must be registered with the Office of the Public Guardianship before it can be used.

You can contact them via www.publicguardian.gov.uk or by calling 0845 330 2900.

Why do I need to think about Inheritance Tax now?

The tax on the estate of a person who has died is called Inheritance Tax. It is dealt with by HM Revenue & Customs (HMRC) (Inheritance Tax). It only applies to a very small percentage of estates. If Inheritance Tax is due, you normally have to pay at least some of the tax before we can issue the grant.

The issue of the grant does not mean that HMRC (Inheritance Tax) have agreed the final Inheritance Tax liability. They will usually contact you again after you have received the grant. Subject to the requirements to pay some of the tax before obtaining the grant, Inheritance Tax is due six months after the end of the month in which the person died. HMRC (Inheritance Tax) will charge interest on unpaid tax from this due date whatever the reason for late payment.

Probate Registry staff are not trained to deal with queries about HMRC forms or Inheritance Tax. If you have any queries about these you should visit the HMRC website: www.hmrc.gov.uk/inheritancetax or contact the Probate and Inheritance Tax Helpline on 0845 30 20 900.

How do I apply for a grant?

You will need to follow the process explained here:

Complete the application form
You will need to complete **Probate Application form PA1, using Guidance Leaflet PA1A**. You can also get these forms from your nearest probate registry or by calling the Probate and Inheritance Tax Helpline – see page 7 for details.

These documents are also available online at hmctsformfinder.justice.gov.uk. You should print off a blank **PA1** and then complete it by hand.

On the application form, you should tell us which Probate Registry interview venue you would like to visit – you can choose the one which is most convenient for you, and any other executors.

Complete the tax form
When you apply for the grant, you will need to complete a tax form **whether or not Inheritance Tax is owed**. You should use form **IHT205** if no Inheritance Tax is owed. If form **IHT205** is not applicable to you, please contact HMRC (Inheritance Tax) for form **IHT400**.

For help completing the forms, you can contact the Probate and Inheritance Tax Helpline (the phone number is on page 7 of this leaflet). You can either work out the Inheritance Tax for yourself or you can ask HMRC to do it for you.

Decide how many official sealed copies of the Grant of Representation you need

Organisations like banks and building societies need to see sealed copies of the grant before they can release assets to you. They won't accept unsealed photocopies.

So if you want to deal with the estate quickly, you may want to order enough sealed copies of the grant to send to all the organisations you are dealing with at the same time.

If there are any assets held outside England and Wales, you may require a special copy of the grant – usually referred to as a sealed and certified copy.

If any person or organisation holding assets insists on seeing an official copy of the grant, you can write to the probate registry, which issued the grant to order more sealed copies. However, these will cost more than those ordered at the time of application (see the fee list), so it's important to decide before you apply for the grant how many copies you will need.

Make sure you enclose the correct documents

You will need to enclose:

- An official copy (**not** a photocopy) of the death certificate issued by the Registrar of Births Deaths and Marriages or a coroner's certificate.

- The **original** will and any codicils (or any document in which the deceased person expresses any wishes about the distribution of his or her estate). Keep a copy of any will or codicil you send us. Please do not attach anything to the will by staple, pin etc. or remove any fastenings from the will.

- Any other documents specifically requested by the Probate Service, such as a decree absolute.

- A cheque made payable to 'HM Courts & Tribunals Service' for the application fee, together with the cost of the number of official sealed grants you require. See the fees list on form **PA3**. (We cannot process your application until the fee has been paid.)

Where should I send my application?

You should send your application to the probate registry of your choice (see leaflet **PA4** for the address). You may wish to send your application by registered or recorded post.

Processing the application

When we receive your application, we will examine it and contact you if there are any queries. If you want us to acknowledge your application, please send a stamped addressed envelope.

If your application is complicated, we may require you to sign additional documents or contact other people – for example, a witness to a will – so that we can interview them or obtain their signatures on documents to help with your application.

If there are no problems, we will send you a letter (usually ten days after we receive your application) inviting you to a 10-15 minute interview at the location you have chosen. This interview is usually held within a month of receiving your application.

If you are applying for a grant with someone else and they cannot come with you, we can arrange for them to attend an interview separately at a different location if necessary. This will, however, delay the time it takes to issue your grant.

What happens at the interview?

The interview is simply to confirm the details you have given on the forms and to answer any queries you or we may have.

We also ask you to sign a form of oath and to swear or affirm before the interviewing officer that the information you have given is true to the best of your knowledge. You will be given the opportunity to swear on the religious book of your choice.

Please bring proof of identification which includes a photograph (such as your driving licence or passport) to the interview. Your appointment letter will tell you about any other identification which is required.

The interview is your chance to tell the interviewing officer if your case is urgent or if you wish to collect the grant in person.

What happens after the interview?

If everything goes smoothly, we will send you the original grant and copies of the grant (if you have requested them) and the original death certificate. The interviewing officer should be able to let you know how long this will take.

If it is not possible to issue a grant, we will explain the reasons.

We retain the original will, as it becomes a public record.

How do I use the grant?

When the grant has been issued you will receive information concerning your role as the executor. You will then have the legal right to ask any person or organisation holding the deceased person's money or property to give you access to these assets. These assets can then be released, sold or transferred as set out in the deceased person's will.

All grants of representation are public records.

The responsibility of the Probate Service ends when the grant is issued, and we cannot advise you on how to administer the estate. If you have any questions about this, you should seek legal advice.

Useful contacts

For general information on wills and probate:
www.direct.gov.uk/death

To access the online forms and leaflets:
hmctsformfinder.justice.gov.uk

To find the addresses of the regional probate registries:
hmctscourtfinder.justice.gov.uk

For information about Inheritance Tax and online forms:
www.hmrc.gov.uk/inheritancetax

For more detailed information about probate and Inheritance Tax:
Probate and Inheritance Tax Helpline: 0845 3020900

Probate forms and leaflets

PA1   Probate application form
PA1A   Probate application form (guidance notes)
PA2   How to obtain probate (leaflet)
PA3   Probate fees list (leaflet)
PA4   Directory of probate registries and interview venues (leaflet)
PA5   Do I need a grant of representation (probate or letters of administration)? (leaflet)
PA6   What will happen at my probate interview? (leaflet)
PA7   How to deposit a will with the Probate Service (leaflet)
PA7A   Withdrawing your will from the Principal Probate Registry (form)
PA8   How to enter a caveat (leaflet)
PA8A   How to enter a caveat (form)
PA9   How to enter a general search (leaflet)
PA10 How to enter a standing search (leaflet)
PA1S Application for a probate search (form)

HMRC Inheritance Tax forms

IHT205 Return of estate information
IHT206 Return of estate information (guidance notes)
IHT400 Inheritance Tax Account

HM Courts & Tribunals Service

PA**4**

Directory of Probate Registries and Appointment Venues

> **For general enquiries, please telephone the Probate and Inheritance Tax Helpline Monday to Friday 9am to 5pm on 0300 123 1072.**
>
> **The main Probate Registries are open to the public 9.30 am to 4.00 pm Monday to Friday. London is open from 10am to 4.30pm Monday to Friday.**

Further information regarding making an appointment to swear your oath will be sent to you by the Probate Registry after you submit your application.

Please note: There is now also an option for you to have your appointment before a commissioner for oaths at a solicitor's office of your choice. Full details of this will also be sent at this stage.

Whichever option you choose your application must be sent to the main Probate Registry. Fees and correspondence can only be taken at the main Probate Registries.

If you have any questions you may contact the Probate Helpline on 0300 123 1072.

Main Probate Registry:	Appointment venues: Opening times of offices marked in bold vary and can be limited. You will be advised of this when we receive your application.
Birmingham Probate Registry The Priory Courts 33 Bull Street Birmingham B4 6DU Tel: 0121 681 3401 Email: birminghamdprenquiries@hmcts.gsi.gov.uk	Birmingham **Nottingham** **Stoke-on-Trent**
Brighton Probate Registry William Street Brighton BN2 0RF Tel: 01273 573510 Email: brightondprenquiries@hmcts.gsi.gov.uk	Brighton **Maidstone**
Cardiff **Probate Registry of Wales** 3rd Floor, Cardiff Magistrates' Court Fitzalan Place, Cardiff South Wales CF24 0RZ Tel: 02920 474373 Email: cardiffdprenquiries@hmcts.gsi.gov.uk	Cardiff **Bristol** **Caernarfon** **Carmarthen** **Bodmin**

Main Probate Registry:	Appointment venues: Opening times of offices marked in bold vary and can be limited. You will be advised of this when we receive your application.
Ipswich Probate Registry Ground Floor 8 Arcade Street Ipswich IP1 1EJ Tel: 01473 284260 Email: Ipswichdprenquiries@hmcts.gsi.gov.uk	Ipswich **Norwich** **Peterborough**
Leeds Probate Registry York House York Place Leeds LS1 2BA Tel: 0113 3896 133 Email: leedsdprenquiries@hmcts.gsi.gov.uk	Leeds **Sheffield** **Lincoln** **York**
Liverpool Probate Registry The Queen Elizabeth II Law Courts Derby Square Liverpool L2 1XA Tel: 0151 236 8264 Email: liverpool.dpr@hmcts.gsi.gov.uk	Liverpool **Chester** **Lancaster**
London Probate Department Principal Registry of the Family Division First Avenue House 42-49 High Holborn London WC1V 6NP Tel: 020 7421 8509 londonpersonalapplicationsenquiries@hmcts.gsi.gov.uk	Central London
Manchester Probate Registry Manchester Civil Justice Centre Ground Floor 1 Bridge Street West PO Box 4240 Manchester M60 1WJ (For Sat Nav purposes the postcode is M60 9DJ) Tel: 0161 240 5701/5702 Email: manchesterdprenquiries@hmcts.gsi.gov.uk	Manchester

Main Probate Registry:	Appointment venues: Opening times of offices marked in bold vary and can be limited. You will be advised of this when we receive your application.
Newcastle-Upon-Tyne Probate Registry Newcastle DPR No 1 Waterloo Square Newcastle-Upon-Tyne NE1 4DR Tel: 0191 211 2170 Email: newcastledprenquiries@hmcts.gsi.gov.uk	Newcastle-Upon-Tyne **Carlisle** **Middlesbrough**
Oxford Probate Registry Combined Court Building St Aldates Oxford OX1 1LY (For Sat Nav purposes the postcode is OX1 1TL) Tel: 01865 793055/793050 Email: oxforddprenquiries@hmcts.gsi.gov.uk	Oxford **Gloucester** **Leicester**
Winchester Probate Registry 1st Floor Southside Offices The Law Courts Winchester Hampshire SO23 9EL Tel: 01962 814100 Email: winchesterdprenquiries@hmcts.gsi.gov.uk	Winchester